# INTEGRAL BUDDHISM

SELECTED BOOKS BY KEN WILBER

Boomeritis
*A Novel That Will Set You Free*

A Brief History of Everything
*20th Anniversary Edition, with a new afterword by*
*Lana Wachowski and Ken Wilber*

Grace and Grit
*Spirituality and Healing in the Life and Death*
*of Treya Killam Wilber*

Integral Meditation
*Mindfulness as a Path to Grow Up, Wake Up,*
*and Show Up in Your Life*

Integral Spirituality
*A Startling New Role for Religion in the Modern*
*and Postmodern World*

The Integral Vision
*A Very Short Introduction to the Revolutionary Integral*
*Approach to Life, God, the Universe, and Everything*

The Religion of Tomorrow
*A Vision for the Future of the Great Traditions—*
*More Inclusive, More Comprehensive, More Complete*

Sex, Ecology, Spirituality
*The Spirit of Evolution*

A Theory of Everything
*An Integral Vision for Business, Politics,*
*Science, and Spirituality*

Trump and a Post-Truth World

# INTEGRAL BUDDHISM

### and the
## Future of Spirituality

## KEN WILBER

SHAMBHALA
*Boulder*
2018

SHAMBHALA PUBLICATIONS, INC.
4720 Walnut Street
Boulder, Colorado 80301
www.shambhala.com

9 8 7 6 5 4 3 2 1

Printed in the United States of America

⊗This edition is printed on acid-free paper that meets the
American National Standards Institute z39.48 Standard.
♻This book is printed on 30% postconsumer recycled paper.
For more information please visit www.shambhala.com.
Distributed in the United States by Penguin Random House LLC
and in Canada by Random House of Canada Ltd

*Library of Congress Cataloging-in-Publication Data*
Names: Wilber, Ken, author.
Title: Integral Buddhism: and the future of spirituality/Ken Wilber.
Description: Boulder: Shambhala, 2018.
Identifiers: LCCN 2017018891 | ISBN 9781611805604
(pbk.: alk. paper)
Subjects: LCSH: Spirituality—Buddhism. | Spirituality. | Buddhism.
Classification: LCC BQ270 .W55 2018 | DDC 294.3/44—dc23
LC record available at https://lccn.loc.gov/2017018891

# CONTENTS

# PREFACE

THE FOLLOWING IS A very short, very introductory—almost
outline summary—of a newly released but much larger and
more detailed book (*The Religion of Tomorrow: A Vision for
the Future of the Great Traditions—More Inclusive, More
Comprehensive, More Complete*). But we felt it was a good
idea, for several reasons, to release this version at this time,
with its basic arguments and core ideas. One is that it was
advisable to have a simplified and easily conveyed version of
the book's main thesis out and available, so important is the
general idea itself. That idea is, basically, that now is absolutely the time that the world's core religions should get serious about updating their fundamental dogmas and dharmas
and gospels—that it has been over a thousand years, at least,
since virtually all of them added significant ideas and practices to their main teachings—teachings that themselves, virtually without exception, were originally created when men and
women literally believed that the earth was flat; that slavery
was considered the normal state of nature; that women and
other minorities were considered second-class citizens, if citizens at all; that evolution had not yet been discovered, nor

most of the modern sciences (and thus the principle source of serious knowledge was considered to be mythic revelation, not scientific experiment); and that the multicultural nature of so much knowledge was completely unheard of. My thesis is that the core ideas of the Great Traditions can literally and seriously be retained, but re-interpreted and included in a much more Inclusive Framework (often called an "Integral Framework") that adds to those core doctrines the many new discoveries about spiritual experience, spiritual intelligence, and spiritual development that have been discovered during those thousand years. The result is a spiritual framework that "transcends and includes" the central teachings of the Traditions, including the old but also adding a significant amount of new material that is fully compatible with the old, but that, in essence, brings it up to date in the modern and postmodern world.

Such updating of Integral approaches to the Great Traditions has already begun in many of them, including Christianity (see, for example, Paul Smith's *Integral Christianity*; Tom Thresher, *Reverent Irreverence*; Bruce Sanguin, *The Emerging Church*; Gary Simmons's work at Unity Church; and the work of Chris Dierkes, Rollie Stanich, Father Thomas Keating, and numerous others), Hinduism (Dustin DiPerna, who has also done significant Integral work on many of the other Great Traditions), Islam (Amir Ahmad Nasr, *My Islam*), Judaism (Marc Gafni's *Radical Kabbalah*), as well as Buddhism (Jun Po Roshi, the dharma heir to Eido Roshi; Jun Po's main student, Doshin; Diane Musho Hamilton; Patrick Sweeney, a lineage heir to Chögyam Trungpa; and Traleg Rinpoche), and in work such as *The Coming Interspiritual Age* (Kurt Johnson and David Ord), to name a few. The excitement caused by such updating has been considerable, particularly considering that it can be done, indeed, while retaining the core teachings of the original Tradition—including ways to rather seamlessly integrate the religious tradition with modern science. This overall approach is achieved by noticing several fundamental items about how spiritual experience and spiritual intelligence are created in the first place, items that were already demonstrably present in the original Teachings, and thus items that can be expanded and updated while not violating the essentials of the original Teachings themselves in the least.

As noted, several teachers have been doing the same thing with Buddhism for several years now, and so it seemed appropriate to summarize the essentials of that new, Integral approach to Buddhism (as an example of how any Great Tradition, in general, can be Integrally updated and informed). As I point out in the beginning chapter of this presentation, Buddhism itself—unlike virtually every other Great Tradition—has always been open to the continuing unfolding and expansion of its own teachings, as evidenced in its own notion of the "Three (or Four) Turnings of the Wheel of Dharma (Truth)," which is a major teaching in Buddhism itself. The idea is that Buddhadharma (Buddhist Truth) has itself already undergone three (or four) major evolutionary Turnings in its own Teachings, according to Buddhism itself. The First Turning began with the original, historical Gautama Buddha himself, and is preserved to this day in teachings such as the Theravada. The Second Turning was introduced by the genius Nagarjuna, around 200 CE, with his revolutionary notion of *shunyata*, or the radical Emptiness or "unqualifiability" of ultimate Reality (which could be said neither to be, nor not to be, nor both, nor neither—the idea being to clear the mind of any and all concepts about Reality so that Reality in itself could be directly experienced), a notion that became the foundation of virtually every Mahayana ("Greater Vehicle") and Vajrayana ("Diamond Vehicle") teaching henceforth. The Third Turning occurred with the half brothers Asanga and Vasubandhu, and is generally called the Yogachara school, sometimes referred to as the "Mind-Only" school (which agreed with Nagarjuna that ultimate Reality was Emptiness, but so was ultimate Mind). This teaching became a central foundation of the great Tantra and Vajrayana (Diamond Path) teachings, which particularly flourished in such places as the extraordinary Nalanda University in India from the 8th to the 11th century CE, and continued unabated in Tibetan Buddhist schools—and, indeed, many Buddhists consider Tantra and Vajrayana to be a "Fourth Turning of the Wheel." (If we do so, which makes sense to me, then what I am actually talking about would be a "Fifth Turning," so please keep that in mind. But whether we acknowledge these Turnings or not doesn't affect the main points of this book, which is what a genuinely inclusive, comprehensive spirituality would begin to look like—this is our main issue.) But with regard to the Turnings, those who acknowledged them maintained that each of them tended to "transcend and include" the previous ones, all of them agreeing with many of the Buddha's original points, and then adding new teachings of their own.

Buddhism is thus used to updating its own major teachings with new and profound additions. But it has been some 1,500 years since the Third Turning; and even the great Tantric schools, which (as noted) flourished from the 8th to the 11th centuries CE, are now close to a thousand years old. The time, again, is more than ripe for a new fundamental addition, a new Turning of the Wheel of Dharma. Many teachers have been saying the same thing for a number of years now; this is one version, a version that has already demonstrated its usefulness and versatility.

This short book is divided into 3 major parts. Part 1 deals with the history of Buddhism and its previous three Turnings. Part 2 briefly describes the new proposed Integral Framework, and demonstrates its fundamental elements and operations. And Part 3 concludes with several musings on the possible future of Buddhism itself, comparing the future of Buddhism if it does become Integral with its future if it doesn't. This future is not dissimilar to that of the other major Traditions themselves: these spiritual systems need to be brought into the modern and postmodern world in significant ways, or face extinction (or, alternatively, become increasingly confined to the childishly minded). The suggestions for how to do so with Buddhism are, in essence, suggestions that can be applied to virtually every other religion; and thus, no matter what your faith (including atheistic or agnostic, and theistic or nontheistic), I believe this book has a good deal to offer you. With humility and gratitude, I therefore offer the following suggestions for ways to return spirituality to the central and fundamental place it has had in human life for most of our existence on earth, although it has, for the last few hundred years, increasingly been losing respect. May this help you locate your own faith (again, atheistic or agnostic, and theistic or nontheistic) in this wondrous, amazing, mysterious, miraculous place we call the Kosmos.

KEN WILBER
Denver, Colorado
Fall 2013

*Part One*

---

# THE PAST

# 1

## HISTORICAL INTRODUCTION

BUDDHISM IS A unique spiritual system in many ways, while also sharing some fundamental similarities with the other Great Wisdom Traditions of humankind. But perhaps one of the most unique features is its understanding, in some schools, that its own system is evolving or developing. This is generally expressed in the notion of the "Three Great Turnings" of Buddhism, or three major stages of unfolding that Buddhism itself has undergone. These three Turnings are, first, Early Buddhism, now generally represented by the Theravada school and thought to contain the historical Gautama Buddha's original teachings, originating in the great Axial period around the 6th century BCE; the Second Turning of the Wheel, represented by the Madhyamika school, founded by Nagarjuna around the 2nd century CE; and the Third (and final, to date) Great Turning of the Yogachara school, originating in the 2nd century CE but having its period of greatest productivity in the 4th century CE with the brothers Asanga and Vasubandhu. As we mentioned, several Buddhists, particularly the Vajrayana schools, consider Tantra and its Vajrayana offshoots to be a "Fourth Turning," which was particularly given form and sophistication at Nalanda University beginning around the 8<sup>th</sup> century CE.

Now the Madhyamika school, although critical of Early Buddhism in many ways, nonetheless transcends and includes many of its foundational teachings, while criticizing those notions it finds partial, limited, or incomplete. And the Yogachara school, particularly the 8<sup>th</sup>-century school called Yogachara-Svatantrika-Madhyamika attempted to integrate and synthesize all three Turnings. The Vajrayana schools likewise contain many of the teachings of the first Three Turnings, and then add their own deeply profound contributions, which, put briefly, focus not only on wisdom and compassion, but also luminosity and numerous skillful means.

In other words, many adherents of Buddhism had a view that Buddhism itself was unfolding, with each new Turning adding something new and important to the overall Buddhist teaching itself. My point can now be put simply: many Buddhist teachers, agreeing with psychologists and sociologists that the world itself, at least in several important ways, is undergoing a global transformation, believe that this transformation will impact Buddhism itself, adding yet newer and more significant truths, and resulting in yet another unfolding, a Fourth Great Turning, of Buddhism. This Fourth Turning retains all the previous great truths of Buddhism, but also adds newer findings from fields as diverse as evolutionary biology and developmental psychology—but all of which are directly and significantly relevant to the field of spirituality itself (i.e., these are not just theoretically and speculatively oriented tack-ons). This new Turning, known by various names—from evolutionary Buddhism to Integral Buddhism—like all the previous Turnings, transcends yet includes its predecessors, adding new material while retaining all essentials. And what is so remarkable about this development is that it is completely in keeping with this general understanding that Buddhism has itself grasped—namely, that Buddhadharma is itself unfolding, growing, and evolving, responding to new circumstances and discoveries as it does so. Even the Dalai Lama has said, for example, that Buddhism must keep pace with modern science or it will grow old and obsolete.

A brief glance at Buddhist history will show what is involved. Original Buddhism was founded on notions such as the difference between *samsara* (the source of suffering) and *nirvana* (the source of Enlightenment or Awakening); the 3 marks of samsaric existence—*dukkha* (or suffering), *anicca* (or impermanence), and *anatta* (or no-self); and the 4 Noble Truths: (1) Life as lived in samsara is suffering; (2) The cause of this suffering is craving or grasping; (3) To end craving or grasping is to end suffering; and (4) There is a way to do so, namely, the eightfold way—of right view, right intention, right speech, right actions, right livelihood, right effort, right mindfulness, and right concentrative absorption.

The ultimate goal of Early Buddhism was to escape samsara entirely—the manifest realm of life, death, rebirth, old age, and sickness—by following the eightfold way and attaining nirvana. "Nirvana" means, essentially, formless extinction. The prefix "nir" means "without," and "vana" has meant everything from desire to grasping to lust to craving for Form itself. The overall meaning is "blown out" or "extinguished." According to some schools, there is even an extreme form of nirvana called *nirodh*—or complete cessation, where neither consciousness nor objects arise at all, and might be thought of as an infinite formlessness. Be that as it may, the goal is clear: get out of samsara and into nirvana.

Such was the basic form of Buddhism as practiced for almost 800 years. Until, that is, Nagarjuna, who began paying attention to this strange duality between samsara and nirvana. For Nagarjuna, there is no ontological difference between samsara and nirvana. The difference is epistemological only. Reality looked at through concepts and categories appears as samsara, while the same Reality looked at free of concepts and categories is nirvana. Samsara and nirvana are not-two, or "nondual"—two different aspects of the same thing. And this caused a major revolution in Buddhist thought and practice.

Nagarjuna relies on the "2 Truths" doctrine—there is relative or conventional truth, and there is absolute or ultimate Truth. Relative truth can be categorized, and is the basis of disciplines such as science, history, law, and so on. That water consists of 2 hydrogen and 1 oxygen atoms is a relative truth, for example. But ultimate Truth cannot be categorized at all. Based on what is known as the "4 Inexpressibles," you can't say that ultimate Reality is Being, nor not-Being, nor both, nor neither. You cannot say it is Self (*atman*), nor no-self (*anatman*), nor both, nor neither. And so on for any category. The reason is that any concept you come up with makes sense only in terms of its opposite (liberated versus bound, infinite versus finite, something versus nothing, implicate versus explicate, pleasure versus pain, and so on)—yet ultimate Reality has no opposite, and thus can't be categorized at all (including that statement). Nagarjuna says, "It is neither void, nor not void, nor both, nor neither, but in order to point it out, it is called the Void." The Void, *shunyata*, or Emptiness. It's a radical "*neti, neti*"—"not this, not that"—except "*neti, neti*" is also denied as a characteristic.

Now what this does mean is that Emptiness, or ultimate Reality, is not separate from anything that is arising. It is the

Emptiness of everything that is arising. Looked at free from conceptualization or categorization, everything that is arising is Emptiness, or Emptiness is the Reality of each and every thing in the manifest and unmanifest world—it is the Suchness or Thusness of each and every thing looked at directly *as it is*, not as it is named, judged, or categorized. Looked at through concepts and categories, the universe appears as samsara—as built of radically separate and isolated things and events, and grasping after those and attachment to them causes suffering. But looked at with *prajna* (nonconceptual awareness), the world of samsara is actually self-liberated nirvana. (In the word "prajna," the "jna," by the way, in English is "kno"—as in "knowledge"—or "gno"—as in "gnosis"—and "pra" is "pro"—so prajna is pro-gnosis, a nondual, unqualifiable knowledge or awareness, which brings Enlightenment or Awakening. Awakening to what? The radical Freedom or infinite Liberation of pure Emptiness, though those terms are at best metaphors.)

Since there is no radical separation between samsara and nirvana (samsara and nirvana being "not-two," or as the *Heart Sutra* summarizes nonduality, "That which is Emptiness is not other than Form; that which is Form is not other than Emptiness"), liberating Emptiness can be found anywhere in the world of Form. One no longer has to retreat to a monastery— away from the world, away from Form, away from samsara— in order to find Liberation. Samsara and nirvana have been joined, united, brought together into a single or nondual Reality. The goal is no longer the isolated saint or arhat, but the socially and environmentally engaged bodhisattva—which literally means "being of Enlightened mind"—whose vow is not to get off samsara and retreat into an isolated nirvana, but to fully embrace samsara and vow to gain Enlightenment as quickly as possible so as to help all sentient beings recognize their own deepest spiritual nature, or Buddhanature, and hence realize Enlightenment.

In one sweep, the two halves of the universe, so to speak—samsara and nirvana—were joined into one, whole, seamless (not featureless) Reality, and Buddhist practitioners were set free to embrace the entire manifest realm of samsara, not avoid it. The vow of the bodhisattva likewise became paradoxical, reflecting both pairs of opposites and not just half—no longer, "There are no others to save," the arhat's chant, but "There are no others to save, therefore I vow to save them all"—reflecting the truth of a samsara and nirvana joined, no longer torn in two.

The Madhyamika notion of Emptiness became the foundation of virtually every Mahayana and Vajrayana school of Buddhism henceforth, becoming—as the title of T. R. V. Murti's book has it, *The Central Philosophy of Buddhism* (although "philosophy" is perhaps not the best word for a system whose goal is to transcend thought entirely).

But there were, nevertheless, still more unfoldings to occur. Particularly by the 4th century CE, the question had become insistent: granted that the Absolute cannot be categorized literally in dualistic terms and concepts, is there really nothing whatsoever that could be said about it at all? At least in the realm of conventional truth, couldn't more systems, maps, models, and at least metaphors be offered about Reality and how to realize it?

Already, in such brilliant treatises as the *Lankavatara Sutra*, the answer was a resounding yes. The *Lankavatara Sutra* was so important it was passed down to their successors by all 5 of the first Chan (or Zen) Head-Founders in China, as containing the essence of the Buddha's teachings. In fact, the early

Chan school was often referred to as the Lankavatara school, and a history of this early period is entitled *Records of the Lankavatara Masters*. (Starting with the 6th Head-Founder, Hui Neng, the *Diamond Sutra*—a treatise solely devoted to pure Emptiness—displaced the *Lankavatara*, and in many ways Zen lost the philosophical and psychological sophistication of the Lankavatara system and focused almost exclusively on non-conceptual Awareness. Zen Masters were often depicted tearing up sutras, which really amounted to a rejection of the 2 Truths doctrine. This was unfortunate, in my opinion, because in doing so, Zen became less than a complete system, refusing to elaborate conventional maps and models. Zen became weak in relative truths, although it brilliantly succeeded in elaborating and practicing ultimate Truth.)

The Yogachara school came to fruition in the 4th century CE with the brilliant half brothers Asanga and Vasubandhu. Asanga was more a creative and original thinker, and Vasubandhu a gifted systematizer. Together they initiated or elaborated most of the tenets of what came to be known as Yogachara (meaning "practice of yoga") or Vijnaptimatra ("consciousness only") school of Buddhism, the Third Great Turning of the Wheel of Dharma.

What all schools of Yogachara have in common is some stance toward the relation of Emptiness and Consciousness. Given the fact that Emptiness and Form are not-two, then Emptiness itself is related to some everyday aspect of Form that the ordinary person is already aware of—in this case, pure Consciousness or unqualifiable everyday Awareness. All schools of Yogachara either equate Emptiness and unconstructed Consciousness directly and ultimately, or at least relatively as a useful orientation and guide for practitioners. For example, the Wikipedia article on Yogachara (I know . . . ) points out both the ultimate and relative view of the connection between Emptiness and Consciousness (or "Mind" with a capital "M"):

> In this view, the Madhyamika position is ultimately true and at the same time the Mind-Only view is a useful way to relate to conventionalities and progress students more skillfully toward the ultimate. . . . [As for the view of an ultimate connection,] while the Madhyamaka held that asserting the existence or non-existence of any ultimately real thing was inappropriate, some exponents of Yogachara asserted that the Mind (or in the more sophisticated versions, primordial wisdom) and only the Mind is ultimately real. Yogachara terminology is also employed by the Nyingmapa [school of Vajrayana Tibetan Buddhism] in attempting to describe the nondenumerable ultimate phenomenon which is the intended endpoint of Dzogchen practice. . . . [The point is that] the ultimate view in both schools is the same [Emptiness or Suchness, or pure, unqualifiable, nondual Empty Awareness], and each path leads to the same ultimate state of abiding.

(One of my favorite stanzas from Tibetan Buddhism summarizes all of this as follows: "All is Mind. Mind is Empty. Empty is freely manifesting. Freely manifesting is self-liberating.")

The Yogachara extends this notion of unconstructed fundamental Consciousness into the idea of 8 (or 9) levels of consciousness, each a transformation of foundational consciousness. The first transformation gives rise to the storehouse consciousness, or the *alaya*. This contains the resultant experiences of all human beings, and the seeds for all future karmic ripening. The second transformation is called (by the *Lankavatara*) the *manas*, which is the self-contraction and self-view, which then looks at the alaya and misinterprets it as a permanent self or soul, and causes the *alaya-vijnana* to become tainted. The third transformation creates the concept of objects—of which, in standard Buddhist psychology, there are 6—the 5 senses, plus the mind (which in Buddhist psychology is treated as another sense) and its conceptual objects (the *manovijnana*), giving us 8 levels of consciousness (or 9 if you count the original, pure, unconstructed Consciousness as such, or primordial empty wisdom).

It's important to realize that for Yogachara, it's not phenomena (or manifest events or the elements of samsara) that cause illusion and suffering, but rather viewing phenomena as *objects*, viewing them through the subject-object duality. Instead of viewing objects as one with the viewer, they are viewed as existing "out there," separate, isolated, dualistically independent, tearing the wholeness of Reality into two realms—a subject versus objects. This—a product of the dualistic self-contraction of the manas and the tainted alaya-vijnana—converts Reality in its Suchness or Thusness or pure Isness into an illusory, broken, fragmented, dualistic world, attachment to which causes bondage and suffering.

This state of bondage, itself illusory, can be seen through by—quoting scholar Sung-bae Park—"a sudden revulsion, turning, or re-turning of the alaya-vijnana back to its original state of purity. The Mind returns to (or is recognized as) its original condition of non-attachment, non-discrimination, and non-duality" (*Buddhist Faith and Sudden Enlightenment* [Albany, NY: SUNY Press, 1983]). In other words, by recognizing the ever-present state of Emptiness. Although most Yogacharins insisted that the end state of Emptiness of the Madhyamika is the same as in Yogachara, there is an unmistakably more positive tone to the Yogachara—certainly in the concept of Mind-Only, but also in how nonduality is conceived. For Madhyamika, nonduality is an utter blank—

at least to the mind's conceptions, although that blankness is actually seeing Reality exactly as it is, in its Suchness or Thusness, without names, concepts, categories, or prejudices. While Yogachara wouldn't specifically disagree, it more positively defines Emptiness and nonduality as "the absence of duality between perceiving subject and the perceived object." Again, it's not phenomena that are illusory or suffering-inducing, but seeing phenomena as *objects*, as items set apart from consciousness or the subject, and existing as independent entities out there. Once they are separated from us, then we can either desire them or fear them, both eventually causing suffering, alienation, and bondage.

Now this slightly more positive view of Emptiness, not to mention its connection to Consciousness (as Zen would put it, following the *Lankavatara Sutra*, "The ordinary mind, just that is the way"), acted to unify Emptiness and Form in an even stronger way than Madhyamika's revolutionary nonduality. And this had a direct hand in the creation of Tantra (and its close cousin, Vajrayana Buddhism), the real flowering of the Third Great Turning.

Tantra was developed primarily at the great Nalanda University in India from the 8th to the 11th centuries CE. For Tantra, what Early Buddhism (and most other religions) considered sins, poisons, or defilements were actually, precisely because of the union of Emptiness and Form, in reality the seeds of great transcendental wisdom. The poison of anger, for example, instead of being denied, uprooted, or repressed, as in so many other approaches, was rather entered directly with nondual Awareness, whereupon it discloses its core wisdom, that of pure clarity. Passion, when entered and embraced with nondual Awareness, transmutes into universal compassion. And so on.

Where the First Turning was the way of renunciation—denying negative states as part of despised samsara—and the Second Turning was the way of transformation—working on a negative state with wisdom until it converted to a positive state—the Third Turning and its Tantric correlate was the way not of renunciation or transformation but the way of transmutation—of looking directly into a negative state of Form in order to directly recognize its already-present state of Emptiness or Primordial Wisdom. The motto here is "Bring everything to the Path." Nothing—absolutely nothing—is taboo—food, alcohol, sex, money—all are to be deeply befriended and lovingly embraced (within, of course, sane limits) as being ornaments of Spirit itself, direct manifestations of the ultimate Divine or Dharmakaya. And all of this because the sacred and the profane, the infinite and the finite, nirvana and samsara, Emptiness and Form, are not two different and separate and fragmented realms, but co-arising, mutually existing, complementary aspects of one Whole Reality, equally to be embraced and cherished.

It was that view, which was a foundation of Tantra and Vajrayana—still prevalent in Tibet (or, alas, the Tibetan community, with Tibet brutally overrun by the Chinese) and truly radical in its nature—that many considered a genuine "Fourth Turning." It was as if the secrets of the world of Form—too long denied, repressed, negatively judged, blamed for all sin and illusion, and ultimately rejected—actually began to give up their divine secrets when viewed as being a manifestation or ornament of Spirit itself. The ultimately wildly Free nature of Emptiness was conjoined with the radically luminous and Full nature of Form (where Emptiness is not something different than Form, but the actual Emptiness *of* all Form) to divulge an infinite Wholeness of self-existing, self-aware, self-liberating, radiant Reality of What there is and All there is, with the secrets of the Form side of the street providing endless new varieties of skillful means (or *upaya*) when directly recognized (*yeshe, rigpa*) as self-liberating Spirit (Svabhavikakaya, or Integrated Body of Truth, and Vajrakaya, or ultimate self-liberating Diamond Truth). Every single phenomenon, when viewed and experienced apart from Spirit, was a source of pain and suffering (*dukkha*), while the same phenomenon, seen as an ornament of Spirit, was a source of potential wisdom, compassion, skillful means, and playful luminosity, all arising as textures of the Primordial Buddha—to give one painfully abbreviated summary of an extraordinarily rich topic.

So, what of a possible New Turning of the Wheel? After Vajrayana and Tantra, where we bring *everything* to the path, what else is possibly left to bring to Buddhism that it doesn't already have? Is this for real, or is it just some inflated, arrogant nonsense?

Well, let's see.

## 2

---

# SOME POSSIBILITIES

W ELL, AS FOR THIS being inflated, arrogant nonsense, we certainly want to be aware of that possibility, and that danger, never underestimating the egotistical tendencies of humankind (yours truly included). But we saw that numerous studies show that a small but significant percentage of the human population is going through a profound transformation. In many ways, it is a global transformation—"global" not just because it is affecting people around the world, but because individual consciousness itself is developing into global dimensions—not egocentric, not ethnocentric, but worldcentric and even Kosmocentric in its identity, its motivations, its desires, its viewpoints and perspectives and capacities.

Nothing like this consciousness has ever existed before in human history—literally. Its impact simply cannot be overestimated. To give one quick example of what's involved: one of the pioneering researchers of this development and the evolution of consciousness was Clare Graves. Graves found that human consciousness moves and develops through around 8 major stages or levels. The first 6 are referred to as 1st tier, or what Maslow called "deficiency needs"—motivation based on lack and scarcity. These levels are all variations on what pioneering developmentalist Jean Gebser called archaic (or instinctual), magic (or egocentric), mythic (or traditional), rational (or modern), and pluralistic (or postmodern). Now what Graves found about these 1st-tier levels is that each level thinks its values and truths are the only real values and truths in the world—all others are infantile, loopy, mistaken, or just plain wrong. With any of those 1st-tier levels in place—which at this particular time in history or evolution covers 95% of the world's population—humanity is destined to disagreement, conflict, terrorism, and warfare. But then Graves found an astonishing fact—at the next basic levels of development, which he called systemic and others have called holistic or integral—there occurs what Graves called "a momentous leap in meaning." The integral levels—or 2nd tier—find some value and partial truth in all of the preceding levels, and it befriends them all in its overall worldview. Its consciousness has indeed become global in its dimensions, including insights and truths from all cultures, all religion, all science—and seeing a profound importance and value in all previous levels—archaic, magic, mythic, rational, and pluralistic. This integral level or levels (some researchers have found 2 or 3 sublevels here) is indeed something radically new in human evolution (it's only a few decades old). While some brilliant pioneering geniuses have demonstrated integral thinking—Plotinus, Shankara, some Yogachara thinkers—for most of human history not more than one-tenth of 1% of the population reached these levels. But over the past several decades, thought leaders in virtually every field of human endeavor have developed these 2nd-tier, integral values, or what Maslow called "Being values," based on abundance, embrace, and inclusion. Up to 5% of the worldwide population has now reached these integral levels, and some developmentalists see this increasing to 10% within the decade. And this, beyond doubt, would change everything.

As a universal growth level, it is a stage to which and through which every human being the world over is destined to grow, if grow they do. This isn't just a mere theory, which you can learn or not learn, or take or leave, but an inherent, universally present stage of human development, like safety, belongingness, and self-esteem. The human race, in other words, is heading toward a world beyond major and deep-seated conflict, and toward one marked more and more often by mutual tolerance, embrace, peace, inclusion, and compassion. Just as an acorn goes through several universal stages on its way to becoming an oak, and an egg goes through several universal stages on its way to becoming a chicken, so a human being goes through several universal stages on its way to maturity, a maturity not characterized by deep-seated conflict and aggression, but now in progress of becoming characterized by deep-seated care and loving-kindness.

All religions, like all other disciplines, will be affected by this profound transformation. And as G. K. Chesterton once quipped, "All religions are the same, especially Buddhism." Buddhism, we have seen, was one of the few religions that from the beginning was marked by evolutionary and integrally inclined thinking, all the way up to the synthesizing Yogachara and Tantra. Yogachara synthesizes all Three Great Turnings. Buddhism is uniquely poised to take the next major step, infused by the coming global Integral transformation, and make its own evolutionary leap forward with a Fourth Great Turning of the Wheel of Dharma and Truth.

What kind of truths would this include? This is what we will be discussing in our next few chapters. But by way of introduction, recall that for Buddhism, Reality is nondual: a not-twoness of samsara and nirvana, finite and infinite, subject and object, Form and Emptiness. Now Emptiness, being void of characterizations (including that one), hasn't changed since the time of the Buddha (in fact, since the Big Bang and before). The experience or recognition of Emptiness is a simultaneous realization, metaphorically, of infinite Freedom, Release, Liberation—liberation from the binding conflict between subject and object and all the torment and torture they inflict on each other. If the experience of Emptiness is one of Freedom, the experience of Form is one of Fullness. And while Emptiness has not changed from the beginning of time, Form has. Form, in fact, has undergone a ceaseless process of evolution, with each stage of evolution adding more and more complexity of Form to the universe, from simple strings to quarks to atoms to molecules to cells to multicellular organisms, with organisms themselves evolving into ever-more-complex forms, from single-celled organisms to photosynthetic plants to animals with neuronal nets, then reptilian brain stems, then limbic systems, then triune brains, whose synaptic connections number more than all the stars in the entire universe.

The same complexification occurred interiorly. Humans, for example (and to return to Gebser's simple terminology), have evolved from simple archaic, to 1st-person magic, to 2nd-person mythic, to 3rd-person rational, to 4th-person pluralistic, to 5th-person and higher integral (1st-, 2nd-, 3rd-, 4th-, and 5th-person refers to the number of perspectives an individual can hold in mind, with the greater the number, the wider and deeper the consciousness doing the holding). The universe of Form, in other words, is becoming Fuller and Fuller. Thus, to reach Enlightenment in today's world—to experience the unity of Emptiness and Form—is not to be any Freer than the great early sages (East and West), since Emptiness is the same, but it is to be Fuller, since the universe of Form has continued to grow and evolve, adding more and more complexity at each point, becoming Fuller and Fuller.

This greater complexity means more and more conventional truths have been discovered, and those need to be taken into account in any Fourth Turning. In Buddha's time, for example, people—including Buddha—really did think the earth was flat. And how could these early sages possibly have known about neurochemistry, about dopamine, serotonin, acetylcholine? Or about the limbic system and its role in emotions, or the reptilian brain stem and its instinctual drives? Likewise, the actual interior stages of development—such as those discovered by Clare Graves, Jean Gebser, or Abe Maslow (which we have been summarizing as archaic, magic, mythic, rational, pluralistic, integral, and super-integral; and we can speak of the same stages using different traits, such as Maslow's needs: physiological needs, safety needs, belongingness needs, self-esteem, self-actualization, and self-transcendence)—these particular types of stages are almost entirely a modern discovery, part of the new complexity evolution brought with the modern era.

We find stages in meditation, stages that are 1st-person or direct experiences and were clearly mapped by the great contemplative traditions East and West (such as St. Teresa's Seven Mansions, the Ten Oxherding pictures of Zen, the stages of Early Buddhism so clearly systematized by Buddhaghosa, Nyingmapa's Nine Yanas, and so on). But these other types of developmental stages—those discovered by figures in modernity, such as Piaget, Baldwin, Graves, Gebser, Maslow, and so on—can't be seen by introspecting, as 1st-person meditative stages can be—because they are 3$^{rd}$-person *structures* discovered by studying large groups of people over long periods of time, and then drawing conclusions about the mental patterns involved.

A famous example is that of Lawrence Kohlberg's work on the growth and development of moral stages, of which he found 6 stages bunched in 3 major groups—pre-conventional (or egocentric), conventional/conformist (or ethnocentric), and post-conventional (or worldcentric). A typical research question behind this discovery was the following: "A man's wife has a terminal illness; the local drugstore has a medicine that will cure her; the man can't afford it; does he have the right to steal it?" Kohlberg found 3 major responses to this question: Yes, No, and Yes. When he asked a person giving the first "Yes," "Why?" the person answered, "Because what's right is what I say is right; if I want to steal it, I'll steal it—and fuck you, by the way." Very egocentric, very self-centered, in other words. When he asked a person giving "No" as a response, "Why?" the person typically answered, "Well, that would be against the law. Society tells me that I can't steal, so I would never do something like that, that would be wrong." This is very group-centered, with "my group, my tribe, my country, right or wrong" being the dominant mode. Very ethnocentric, in other words, very group-oriented. Finally, when he asked the person giving the second "Yes," "Why?" he typically got things like, "Well, life is worth more than $27, so in this case, yes, of course I'd steal it to save a life." Very universally oriented, highly principled, very worldcentric. And further—and this is what makes these stages a developmental sequence—if a person ever switched stages, it was always in a higher direction, either from the first egocentric "Yes" to ethnocentric "No," or from ethnocentric "No" to the second, worldcentric "Yes." In other words, there is a directionality here, and it is always from egocentric to ethnocentric to worldcentric, and these stages can neither be skipped nor reversed.

Literally hundreds and hundreds of research projects have investigated these types of stages of development. We now know that there are multiple intelligences—not just cognitive intelligence, but also emotional intelligence, moral intelligence, intrapersonal intelligence, aesthetic intelligence, interpersonal intelligence, mathematico-logical intelligence, and so on. And as different as these intelligences are—they are also called developmental *lines*—what research shows is that they all develop through the same basic developmental *levels* (which we have been referring to as archaic, magic, mythic, rational, pluralistic, integral, and super-integral). In the book *Integral Psychology*, I give charts containing over 100 different developmental models—each dealing with a particular multiple intelligence or developmental line—and again, what is so remarkable is the astonishing similarity of the developmental *levels* they all go through.

In whatever intelligence or line, an infant generally starts out in a state of fusion or indissociation with the surrounding world—it can't tell where its self ends and the environment begins. (This is the Archaic View.) At around 18 months—which is actually called "the psychological birth of the infant"—just that happens: the infant develops a separate emotional self that it can distinguish from its surroundings. The thought process here is still often fused with the environment, what Freud called primary process thinking, and hence is very fantasy-dominated and superstitious: if I wish my father dead, and he dies, it was my thinking that actually caused his death. (This is the Magic View.) As concepts begin to emerge, the mind begins to differentiate from the body—if this goes too far into dissociation, then we have the standard repression of various bodily impulses and feelings (sex, aggression, power, etc.). Thinking is impulsive, "if I see something I want, I take it," and it is dominated by individuals that are mythically exaggerated beings, "if I can no longer perform magic, they can." If mommy wanted, she could change this yucky spinach into candy. And God or the Goddess or some other supernatural heavenly being knows everything I'm thinking and will punish me for bad thoughts. (This is the emergence of the Mythic View.) Since it's the beginning of the emergence of the capacity for group thinking, and identifying with groups—my family, my clan, my tribe, my religion, my nation—it tends to be very conventional and conformist, as with the "No" response in the Kohlberg example.

By the time of adolescence, thought begins to operate on thought, and we get the emergence of the rational stage of development—in cognition, in morals, in interpersonal intelligence, and in any other multiple intelligence in which reason begins to emerge. Self-esteem begins to replace belongingness and peer pressure as a basic motivation, and scientific thinking becomes possible and common. (This is the Rational View.) It tends to mark the switch from very conformist types of thinking to very reflective and critical thinking—criticizing and judging my culture, my thoughts, my ideas, my values. If development continues, by early adulthood, thought begins to operate on this rational thinking itself, and starts to see many other viewpoints than the merely rational or scientific one. The importance of culture in creating interpretations of Reality becomes significantly noticed and emphasized, and a multicultural, many-valued stage emerges, known generally as the Pluralistic (or Postmodern) View. This View famously sees separate, isolated, discontinuous cultures and ideas and individuals, and finds very few common or universal traits or phenomena—so much so, the world becomes a fragmented, disjointed, partial, and broken affair, and it's not until the emergence of a higher, broader, wider mode of cognition (2$^{nd}$ tier or Integral) that awareness can look at all of the broken fragments and start to find universal, uniting, common patterns that connect various cultures, individuals, and phenomena in general. This is the Integral View, in whatever intelligence it shows up, and this marks the emergence that Clare Graves referred to as that "monumental leap in meaning"— from broken and fragmented to unified and synthesizing. And if development continues (into Super-Integral stages), Awareness itself starts to become transpersonal, spiritual, universal, Kosmocentric, connected to various types of direct spiritual experience (which we will return to in more detail later).

Now the point about this developmental sequence, which consists of various *structures* of consciousness, is that they are not generally items that can be seen by simply introspecting. Thus, these types of stages are rarely found in meditation maps, which deal instead in various *states* of consciousness that can be directly seen and felt by introspecting. If you are sitting on a meditation mat, you will never have an experience that, for example, says, "This is a moral-stage-3 thought." But you can directly experience, say, the second major stage of mahamudra meditation, the direct, immediate experience of luminosity and various phenomena of light. These are clear and directly obvious and immediately experienced, whereas the structure-stages of various multiple intelligences are deduced from experience by studying large groups of people over long stretches of time. And this is why none of the typical developmental stages found by modern developmental psychology are found in any of the maps of meditation left by the Great Wisdom Traditions from around the world—and why these particular *structures* of consciousness need to be included in any of the maps of meditative *states* of consciousness left us by the world's contemplative traditions.

And there's another important reason both of these need to be included. For what developmentalists have discovered is that things like $1^{st}$-person meditative *states* (or *state*-stages) are interpreted according to the $3^{rd}$-person *structure*-stage one is at. For example, Buddhism can be—and is—interpreted at magic levels, mythic levels, rational levels, pluralistic levels, and integral levels. In Part 2, I'll give specific examples of Buddhist thinkers and entire schools that are coming from magic, mythic, rational, pluralistic, and integral levels.

This means—and this would be part of the understanding of any new and Integral Fourth Turning—that we actually have 2 major axes of spiritual development. In addition to meditative *states* of consciousness—starting with gross egoic thoughts, moving through subtle illumination and insight, and culminating in a nondual Great Perfection—we have the growth of *structures* of consciousness (such as magic to mythic to rational to pluralistic to integral), and a person will largely interpret the meditative-state experience according to the structure of the major stage of development they are at. Structures are also responsible, as we have seen, for the patterns of our major multiple intelligences (cognitive intelligence, emotional intelligence, moral intelligence, aesthetic intelligence, and so on, all of which are composed not of states but of structures). Structures are how we GROW UP; states are how we WAKE UP. Any Fourth Turning would want to take both of those forms of growth into account (whereas, at this point in time, there's not a single growth technology, East or West, that includes both structures and states in overall growth and development, spiritual or otherwise).

(As for structures of consciousness, and their stage development, the evidence is overwhelming. As mentioned earlier, in a book I wrote entitled *Integral Psychology*, there are charts that show over 100 different systems of developmental studies, and the remarkable thing is that virtually all of them are in a similar general agreement as to the major structure-stages a human develops through [and which I just summarized above]. This is a little-known, yet profound discovery, and has enormous impact on how we view humans, their views of the world, and their capacities for growth and development. Given that structures are the mental tools through which we see and interpret the world, including various state experiences, such as meditation, their importance for any spiritual system becomes quite apparent. [More about this when we discuss structures in greater detail.])

Likewise, discoveries about the personal repressed shadow elements in a human are largely a modern discovery. Meditation can loosen the repression barrier and make shadow access easier. But this isn't always a good thing, and in some cases makes them worse. Most meditation, for example, works by helping us dis-identify or detach from the body and mind, from personal thoughts, feelings, and emotions. But much psychopathology stems from a premature or overdone detachment or dissociation or dis-owning of specific thoughts or feelings. Anger, for example, can be dissociated or dis-owned, frequently causing feelings of sadness or depression. In meditation, if I am dis-identifying with whatever arises, I will simply further dis-own this anger, making my depression worse. The only advice the meditation teacher has for me is "Intensify your efforts!" which really makes it worse.

Regrettably, it's still the case in many religions that if you have an emotional problem or shadow issue, you are simply thought not to be practicing the religion hard enough. You either aren't practicing enough *vipassana*, or you don't believe fervently enough in Jesus, or you haven't found the right relation to Torah, and so on.

Adding some simple and widely accepted psychotherapeutic techniques to meditation practice can not only help handle any shadow elements, but make meditation itself cleaner and more efficient and effective. Some simple shadow procedures, too, would be a welcome addition to any Fourth Turning.

In the next section, we'll discuss these "3 S's"—structures of consciousness, states of consciousness, and shadow elements—and how their inclusion would be a beneficial component of any Fourth Turning or Integral Spirituality.

*Part Two*

---

# THE PRESENT

# 3

## VIEWS AND VANTAGE POINTS

W E HAVE BEEN talking about the three major Turnings of the Wheel of Dharma that Buddhism itself recognizes. The First Turning is Early Buddhism, the original teachings of the historical Gautama the Buddha. Generally thought to be represented by Theravada Buddhism, it is particularly prevalent in Southeast Asia, and has recently found fans in the West. The Second Great Turning is represented by Nagarjuna and the Madhyamika school of Buddhism, which presented the notion of shunyata, or Emptiness, a profound elaboration of the nature of ultimate Truth that became fundamental to virtually every school of subsequent Buddhism, Mahayana and Vajrayana. And the Third Great Turning, that of Yogachara or Vijnanavada Buddhism, which is associated with the brothers Asanga and Vasubandhu, and often referred to as the Mind-Only or representation-only school, which was particularly influential in the Vajrayana and Tantric schools.

As those three unfoldings developed, there was an increasing drive to integrate or synthesize all of them, and some fairly successful attempts ensued. Buddhism has always had a strong synthesizing tendency, and there are today a growing number of Buddhist teachers and students who feel enough new truths have emerged that need to be integrated into Buddhism that we are on the verge of yet another unfolding, a Fourth Great Turning of the Wheel. What follows are a few thoughts on some of the more important items that would be included in this new synthesis, a notion that will be continued in chapter 4 as well.

## STATES AND STRUCTURES

*States* of consciousness have been generally known by humankind for thousands of years. As 1st-person, direct, immediate experiences, they are open to introspection, meditation, vision quest, and other direct experiential modes. *Structures* of consciousness, on the other hand, are the implicit, embedded, 3rd-person mental patterns or structures through which the mind views and interprets the world, including states. Things like multiple intelligences are made of mental structures. Things like experiences, religious experiences, day-to-day feelings, and meditative states are made of, well, states. And, as I said, since states of consciousness are direct, immediate, 1st-person experiences, they have been understood, or at least known, for thousands of years; whereas structures, as implicit, embedded, 3rd-person patterns that are not usually looked at but looked through, have to be deduced from experimental setups, and thus weren't really known or understood until the modern era, a few hundred years ago at most. And yet both are absolutely crucial for understanding the mind, awareness, consciousness, and the mind's functioning, in everything from worldviews to spirituality to science.

## STATES AND VANTAGE POINTS

Let's start with states of consciousness. The great contemplative traditions generally list 4 or 5 major, natural states of consciousness, available to all humans virtually from birth forward. These are waking, dreaming, deep formless sleep, Witnessing or unqualifiable Awareness, and nondual awakened Suchness. Dream and deep sleep are not confined to sleeping. The dream state includes subtle or bioenergy, mental states, and higher mental states such as creativity and idealizing and synthesizing. And the deep-sleep state, when viewed as its own state and not combined with Witnessing, is simply the very first point or realm where ultimate unmanifest Reality first becomes manifest, and thus it is the home of the very first, most subtle forms of existence—space and time, for example, and the collective storehouse consciousness. Sometimes it's combined with pure Emptiness, or unqualifiable Awareness as such, and then the subtle becomes the first manifest realm. This gives us 4 major states or realms instead of 5, and the 5 standard realms of matter, body, mind, soul, and spirit are reduced to 4: body, mind, soul, and spirit—known in Buddhism, for example, as the Nirmanakaya, Sambhogakaya, Dharmakaya, and Svabhavikakaya. These realms are also known as the gross physical realm, the subtle mind realm, the causal Witnessing or Real Self realm, and the ultimate Spirit or nondual Suchness or Unity realm, whose correlative states of consciousness include, respectively, the waking state, the dream state, the formless or empty Witnessing state, and the ultimate ever-present nondual Spirit or Suchness Awareness state.

Now, Consciousness or Wakefulness starts out identified with the gross waking state. The goal of meditation is to discover pure Emptiness, the void Godhead, Ayin, pure

Nothingness or the Plenum/Void—by whatever name—and thus cease identifying with the small, finite, mortal, skin-bounded ego and find instead what the Sufis call the Supreme Identity, or Zen calls our Original Face, or Christians call Christ Consciousness—our True Self and ultimate nondual Spirit that is radically free from an identity to any particular finite thing or event whatsoever—or, put from another angle—is one with absolutely the entire manifest and unmanifest realm, radically One with the All, One with the entire Ground of Being. Being one with everything that arises moment to moment, there is literally nothing outside of us that we could want or desire, nor anything outside of us that we could smash into—thus no fear, no anxiety, no angst. As the Upanishads say, "Wherever there is other, there is fear"—but when we are one with All, there is no Other that is not our own True Self, and thus we are liberated, enlightened, free from torment and suffering and Awakened to the ultimate Goodness, Truth, Reality, and Beauty—unborn and undying, unbounded and unlimited, fiercely free and alive, joyously One and blissfully All, radiantly infinite and timelessly eternal—a state known variously as Enlightenment, Awakening, *moksha* (or liberated), *metanoia* (or transformed), *wu* (or transparently Open, Free, and Full).

Now between our original starting point—where our Consciousness or Wakefulness is exclusively identified with the gross waking state—and our final liberation—where our Wakefulness is identified with pure Empty Suchness or nondual Unity—there are 4 or so states of consciousness that are less-than-fully Awakened. Each of these states constitutes an identity that is, so to speak, deeper and higher and closer to the ultimate nondual Supreme Identity, but not quite there—although, again, each state gets a bit closer and closer. And the aim of meditation is to move through these states in Awareness or in Consciousness or in Wakefulness—transcending and including all of them—or moving through each, first identifying with it in Wakefulness, and then transcending or dis-identifying with it as we move to the next deeper or higher state, until we have transcended or moved beyond all of them to the ultimate nondual state, and yet include all of them in our Awareness. So we have transcended or moved beyond *all* of them—we are identified with nothing, absolutely nothing, or pure Emptiness—and we have included or identified with *all* of them as well—we are both nothing and everything, Emptiness and the All, radical Freedom and overflowing Fullness, zero and infinity. We have discovered our Real Self, one with Spirit, which is the Self of the entire Kosmos as well. We have, indeed, come Home.

Now every great meditative tradition the world over has major maps of the significant steps or stages in meditation as their tradition has come to understand and practice them. And what significant research has demonstrated is that, although the surface features of each of these traditions and their stages differ considerably from culture to culture, the deep features of all of them are in many ways significantly similar. In fact, virtually all of them follow the 4 or 5 major natural states of consciousness given cross-culturally and universally to all human beings—gross, subtle, causal, Witnessing, and Suchness (we'll discuss the specific meaning of those terms in a moment—for now, they are variations on waking, dreaming, deep sleep, witnessing, and nondual).

In Integral Theory, there's something we refer to as the self's "center of gravity." The self has two of these—its *"structure center of gravity"* (or where, on the overall spectrum of structures and their growth—or structure-stages—the self is most identified at a given point), and the "*state* center of gravity" (or where, on the spectrum of major states and one's growth through them—or state-stages—the self is most identified). So, in the structure growth process—archaic to magic to mythic to rational to pluralistic to integral to super-integral—one might be mostly at the mythic level, while in state development—gross to subtle to causal to witnessing to nondual—one might be mostly at subtle. One's dual center of gravity, then, would be (mythic, subtle).

This relationship is often referred to as the Wilber-Combs Lattice, after myself and Allan Combs, who independently came up with essentially the same idea (see fig. 3.1). Up the vertical axis in that figure is any representative of structure growth (in any multiple intelligence). We're using our standard archaic, magic, mythic, rational, pluralistic, integral, and super-integral levels. Across the top are any major states of consciousness being considered. In this case, 4 of our standard 5 major states—the gross, subtle, causal, and nondual (and under those are the names of mystical peak experiences of those states—oneness with the entire gross realm being nature mysticism; oneness with a subtle Deity Form being deity mysticism; oneness with the formless causal/witnessing state is formless mysticism; and oneness with the ultimate nondual realm is nondual or unity mysticism). And the important central point about this figure is that, as indicated, each major state will be interpreted (and therefore experienced) from a basic structure (archaic to super-integral). Depending upon which structure-stage a person is at, this will change dramatically the nature and experience of each of these states (either in themselves, or as a particular state-stage in an overall path of meditation). We'll return to this when we give examples of Buddhism at each structure and how each one differently

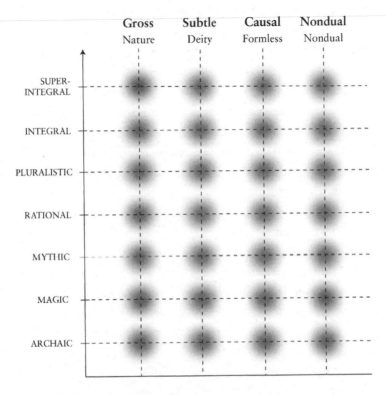

FIGURE 3.1. *The Wilber-Combs Lattice.*

interprets its own teachings. But first, let's look at the evidence for the existence of these 5 major states and their stages in all of the world's great contemplative systems.

Now instead of giving a ton of examples of the similarities in deep features of the world's meditative traditions, I'll just give 3 or 4 from the East, the West, and postmodernity.

First, let's look at a very simplified overview summary of what's involved. No matter what structural center of gravity a person has when he or she starts meditation (from magic to integral), they almost always will start with a state center of gravity at the gross waking state. (Now the structure center of gravity is definitely important, because it will largely determine how the various meditative state-stages are interpreted. But we'll come back to that.)

Statewise, at the gross waking realm, the individual is identified with the physical body and the gross-reflecting mind— the gross, chaotic, "monkey mind"—the stream of thoughts, feelings, emotions, and sensations centered on the egoic state and reflecting the material realm and its desires. In mindfulness forms of meditation, the person is told to simply witness the stream of events, without judgment, condemnation, or identification. After several months of this, the monkey mind will begin to calm down, and one's awareness will open to subtler dimensions of mind and being—perhaps subtle states of loving-kindness, states of luminosity and almost infinite illumination, stretches of profoundly peaceful stillness and mental quiet, experiences of expanding beyond the ego into deeper and deeper states of I AMness (at this stage, often referred to as the subtle soul; as for "soul," Buddhists should realize that, like the ego, the soul has merely a conventional reality, not an ultimate reality; but at this state-stage, as with the ego at the gross-state/realm, the soul has a *conventionally* real reality, an exclusive identity with which will eventually have to be died to). As meditative awareness deepens into the causal/witness itself, stretches of pure awareness free of thought altogether can increase; states of transpersonal identity or True Self or infinite I AMness can increasingly occur; universal love, bliss, happiness, and joy can arise; identity with the finite bodymind can drop altogether, to be replaced with anything from Christ Consciousness to Buddhamind to Ein Sof. And if awareness deepens even further, from causal/witnessing to ultimate unity or nonduality, the sense of subject-object duality—the sense of a Witness or Looker witnessing phenomena—drops out entirely, and instead of looking at a mountain, you are the mountain; instead of feeling the earth, you are the earth; instead of being aware of clouds floating by in the sky, the clouds float by in *you*, in your own awareness. As a Zen Master put it upon his awakening, "When I heard the sound of the bell ringing, there was no bell and no I, just the ringing." When that state becomes more or less permanent, one's state center of gravity has gone from gross to subtle to causal/witnessing to nondual suchness—and you *are* the Supreme Identity—one with Spirit, and one with the entire manifest world (whatever it is that the world consists of for you—which, as we will see, changes and expands from structure to structure to structure).

Evelyn Underhill, in her classic book *Mysticism*, points out that virtually all Western mystics progress through the same general 4 or 5 major state-stages on their way to permanent realization—and they are, of course, variations on the standard gross, subtle, causal formless, and nondual unity. But let me first point out that state development, unlike structure development, is much looser and less rigid. Structures are, well, more structured—they emerge in an order that can't be changed by social conditioning; you can't skip structure-stages; and you can't peak experience structures higher than a stage or so away (unlike states). Somebody at moral-stage 1, for example, can't peak experience a moral-stage-5 thought. But somebody at a gross state can peak experience a causal or even Nondual state. And mindfulness meditation has you start out by identifying (or at least trying to identify) with Witnessing awareness (although it's still true that, on balance, one's state center of gravity itself will permanently shift stage by stage, since actual identification, as opposed to temporary peak experiences, with higher states rests on certain previous identities with junior states; nonetheless, even that is not a hard-and-fast rule).

But with that in mind, Underhill's stages are gross purgation—where one works with purifying and releasing identity with the physical body and its thoughts; subtle illumination, where one is introduced to all the subtler dimensions, luminosities, and higher emotions of the soul; a dark night, where one discovers a causal, formless cloud of unknowing, a liberation from finite bondage (and one often suffers terribly as this vast Freedom is lost because realization is not yet permanent); and finally a nondual unity consciousness, where soul and God disappear into ultimate Godhead. The whole process is often initiated with a peak experience of awakening or metanoia, a glimpse that shows one the Paradise of ultimate Reality and sets the soul on the Path of state-stages and Waking Up. In a book I co-authored called *Transformations of Consciousness*, we included a chapter by the Harvard theologian John Chirban, who used, as examples, early church desert saints, showing that all of them went through around 5 state-stages, all variations on Underhill's 4 or 5 basic stages (and those all variations on gross, subtle, causal, witnessing, and nondual).

Speaking of *Transformations of Consciousness*, one of my main co-authors for that book, Daniel P. Brown, also of Harvard, has spent the last 30 years of his life studying the meditation systems of the world, focusing on one of the most sophisticated and complete systems ever devised, the mahamudra system of Tibetan Buddhism. Working with 14 root mahamudra texts, all in their original language, he showed they each went through the same essential 4 or 5 stages of development (stages he calls Vantage Points). Now a Vantage Point is to a state/realm what a View is to a basic structure-rung. Let's briefly look at what that means and then return to our main topic.

In structure development, we have a metaphor we call "ladder, climber, View." The ladder is the spectrum of basic structures of consciousness, or the basic rungs in the ladder. Once they emerge, they stay in existence. I'll give examples of these in a minute. The climber is the self-system. As it climbs the basic rungs of existence, it temporarily and exclusively identifies with each rung in turn and sees the world through the eyes of that rung. In other words, its View of the world is determined by that rung and its characteristics. For example, when it identifies with the concrete mind, it sees the world in concrete mythic-literal terms. When it identifies with the rational mind, it sees the world in modern, rational, scientific, or objective terms. When it identifies with synthesizing vision-logic, it creates an Integral View. And so on. Figure 3.2 is an abbreviated list of basic rungs or basic structures and their corresponding Views—or the way the world looks when a structure becomes a structure-stage, or where that particular structure-rung has been identified with by the self and thus it becomes the self's structure center of gravity through which it views and interprets the world. (Views are what we have been calling things like archaic, magic, mythic, rational, pluralistic, integral, and super-integral.) Figure 3.2 shows the corresponding basic rungs supporting those Views. (Note: As for the names of the Views, the ones we have been using—such as magic and pluralistic, or belongingness and self-esteem—are simply a few names taken from a couple of multiple intelligence lines; there are literally dozens of different names we could use for each View, so keep in mind these are a very narrow selection of possible terms for Views.)

| | RUNG (*structure*) | VIEW (*structure-stage*) |
|---|---|---|
| Fulcrum-1 | sensorimotor mind | Archaic |
| Fulcrum-2 | instinctual or impulsive mind | Magic; emotional-sexual |
| Fulcrum-3 | conceptual or intentional mind | Magic-mythic; power |
| Fulcrum-4 | concrete mind | Mythic; conformist; traditional; belonging |
| Fulcrum-5 | rational mind | Reason; multiplistic; modern; self-esteem |
| Fulcrum-6 | pluralistic mind | Pluralistic; post-modern; planetary |
| Fulcrums-7 | low and high vision-logic; | Holistic; systemic |
| and 8 | $2^{nd}$-tier or systemic mind | Integral; global |
| Fulcrums-9 | meta-mind | Transglobal |
| 10 | $3^{rd}$ para-mind, super-integral | Visionary |
| 11 | tier overmind | Transcendent |
| 12 | supermind | Transcendent-Immanent; Nondual |

FIGURE 3.2. *Basic structure-rungs and their correlative views.*

During the course of structure and structure-stage development, as the self or climber steps from one stage to the next higher stage, 2 important things happen: (1) The self drops or loses the View from the lower rung and replaces it with the View from the next rung. Obviously, when you're climbing a ladder and you move from, say, rung 3 to rung 4, you are no longer looking at the world from rung 3—that View is gone. You are instead looking at the world from rung 4. But (2) rung 3 itself still remains in existence—in fact, rung 4 is resting on it. So in each stage of structure development, the basic rung remains in existence and is included, but the View from that rung is lost, transcended, negated; it is replaced by the View from the next higher rung as the self exclusively identifies with that. This is what we mean when we say development is to transcend and include, or negate and preserve (as Hegel put it, "To supersede is at once to negate and to preserve," which we usually translate as "transcend and include"). What is preserved and included are the basic structure-rungs; what is negated and transcended are the particular Views. Each time one of these major transformations occurs, we call it a "fulcrum" of development; 12 such fulcrums, corresponding with 12 major structure-rungs, are given in fig. 3.2.

Now the same transcend and include occurs with states and their realms, with the view or Vantage Point from those state-realms as the central self develops through those state-realms, successively identifying and then dis-identifying its exclusive state identity from state-stage to state-stage to state-stage (or shifts its state center of gravity from state-stage to state-stage). State-realms are preserved and included; Vantage Points are transcended and negated. By way of introduction to these successive state-stages, Geshe Kelsang Gyatso gives the following 6 stages to mahamudra meditation:

1. Identifying our own gross mind
2. Realizing our gross mind directly
3. Identifying our subtle mind
4. Realizing our subtle mind directly
5. Identifying our causal/nondual mind
6. Realizing our causal/nondual mind directly

(Here, Gyatso uses the standard 3-state/realm summary—Nirmanakaya, Sambhogakaya, and Dharmakaya—or gross, subtle, and very subtle [the Tibetan term for "causal" is "very subtle"—so instead of "gross, subtle, causal," it's "gross, subtle, very subtle"]; this 3-state summary implicitly collapses the 4th-state witnessing mind and the 5th-state nondual empty mind—both of which are recognized by the Tibetans, but they often include them in the Dharmakaya or very subtle [or "causal"], which I have therefore summarized as causal/nondual. This is simple semantics. The point is that "gross, subtle, causal" is well-recognized by this Tradition.)

Dan Brown starts with the gross waking state, where the average person is exclusively identified with the gross physical body and gross thoughts and feelings. After various preliminaries and meditation practice gets under way, the first major shift is from the gross state-stage and its Vantage Point to the subtle state-stage and its Vantage Point. Here, one is no longer exclusively identified with the physical body and thoughts, or the gross realm in general (although, like basic rungs, this major state-realm remains in existence), but the central self is now identified with the subtle realm and its Vantage Point, which is no longer the gross ego but what Brown calls the subtle personality (what Christian contemplatives call the "soul"). Brown calls this stage "Awareness," since it is the first stage free of gross rambling thoughts and emotions, and is more in touch with pure Awareness. At the next state-stage, the causal state-stage, the subtle personality, soul, or Vantage Point is dismantled (although the subtle realm itself remains in existence), and what remains are the very subtlest (or "causal") forms of manifestation itself—namely, space and time. Dan calls this causal stage "Awareness-itself." As development continues into the next state-stage, that of Witnessing awareness, one ceases to identify exclusively with the causal and its Vantage Point, and instead transcends space and time to find a pure timeless Now—and an Awareness that focuses on the pure Present. Brown calls this "Awareness-in-and-of-itself." It's also at this point that 3 sublevels of nonduality emerge (recognizing nonduality after a thing arises, while it arises, and before it arises, only the last one of which is true Enlightenment or Awakening). This is Brown's last major stage—Awakened nondual Awareness, which sheds the subject object duality that subtly remained with the Witness (and which Brown calls "individuality"—which is often referred to as the True Self or Real Self—an "individuality" that finally must be transcended for ultimate nondual unity or Suchness), which sees the world as a seamless (not featureless) Wholeness, or nondual Reality, where a person's Awareness is one with all gross, subtle, and causal phenomena, but exclusively identified with none of them. Those realms continue to exist and arise, but not an exclusive identity or attachment to any of them. (Thus, gross, subtle, causal, witnessing, and nondual.)

To give a final, postmodern example, we have the American adept Adi Da, who maintains, "To Realize Most Perfect Divine Enlightenment, the ego must be transcended through three distinct phases—first at the [gross] physical level (the level of "money, food, and sex"), then at the subtle level (the level of internal visions, auditions, and all kinds of mystical experience), and finally at the causal level (the root-level of conscious existence, wherein the sense of "I" and "other," or the subject-object dichotomy, seems to arise in Consciousness)." The fourth phase for Adi Da is the Realization of "Always-Already Truth," the ever-present Goal, Ground, and Condition of all existence, high or low, sacred or profane, manifest or unmanifest—thus, gross, subtle, causal (implicit root witnessing), nondual.

A simple summarizing schematic of the 5 major states and state-stages of meditation are given in figure 3.3. Evelyn Underhill's stages are given in italics on the left of the diagram, representing the West; stages of yet another Eastern system—Highest Yoga Tantra—are listed in the "southeast" line of the diagram (starting with "5 skandhas," or 5 major forms of gross consciousness—material form, image, symbol, conceptual mind, and egoic self-concept—and ending with "black near-attainment," or the causal "blackness" or Abyss-nature preceding nondual Awakening). The major state-stages are gross, subtle, causal, *turiya* (which means literally "the fourth," as in the 4th major state of consciousness, that of the Witness), and finally *turiyatita* ("beyond the fourth"), or nondual Awakened Awareness. Each of the major state-stages has a "dark night" listed, which involves, among other things, the death of the particular separate self-sense associated with that state-realm, from the ego of the gross, to the soul of the subtle, to the Witness of the causal/witnessing, on the way to the purely unqualifiable nondual Awakened Awareness or Suchness. (Failure to differentiate from and dis-identify with a particular self-sense results in a fixation/addiction to that self; going too far and dissociating and dis-owning the particular self-sense results in an avoidance/allergy to that self. Both are malformations of development—misnavigations of "transcend and include"—and constitute serious dysfunctions in overall state evolution.) The point of the overall meditative path is to have Wakefulness (or Consciousness as Such) transcend and include all state-realms, so it ceases to "black out" or "forget" various changes of state (such as dreaming and deep sleep), and instead recognizes a "constant Consciousness" or ever-present nondual Awareness, the union (and transcendence) of individual finite self and infinite Spirit.

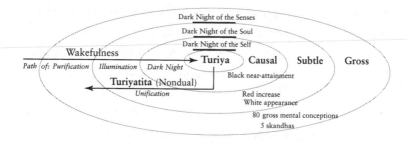

FIGURE 3.3. *Major stages of meditative states.*

These universal similarities are likely rooted in, or at least correlated with, the natural states of consciousness that the brains of all human biological organisms are born with— gross waking, subtle dreaming, causal deep formless sleep, plus ever-present nondual Awareness, source and support of them all. Postmodernists who try to explain away all universals have a hard time explaining away these universal brain states. Trying to maintain that Buddhists have culturally constructed major brain states that are massively different from Jewish brain states which are different from Hindu brain states just doesn't make sense. Our biological brains and their states are similar in deep features wherever humans appear, and hence contemplative and meditative stages take on a universal character (again, in their deep features, whereas their surface features differ from culture to culture and often individual to individual).

The stages of meditation, in other words, like virtually everything else, are a 4-quadrant affair (the 4 quadrants are 4 major perspectives inherent in any situation, and which we will return to in a moment). These include areas such as biological, psychological, cultural, and social factors—all of which will play a role in how the surface features of these meditative stages appear and are experienced. It's fairly well-recognized that cultural and social factors play an important role in how human experience unfolds. (This is true for transpersonal universal features as well—they are interpreted by structures in all 4 quadrants. Thus, for example, it is common to find in Western mystical literature innumerable references to beings of light, often with 2 wings—in other words, angels. But there is not a single mention of a being of light with 10,000 arms; and yet that is an incredibly common sight in Tibet, representing the bodhisattva of compassion, Avalokitesvara, of whom, for instance, the Dalai Lama is said to be an incarnation. The point is not that these figures are merely cultural constructions—the subtle consciousness state and the brain state from which they both originate are very real, and found universally; but they are interpreted by factors that include cultural and social molding factors.)

What is less often—in fact, rarely—understood is the importance of Views and Vantage Points in determining human experience—how it is seen and how it is interpreted and experienced. These Views and Vantage Points are every bit as real as cultural and social factors.

States and their realms—gross, subtle, causal/witnessing, and nondual—determine the types of phenomena in general that can arise to be experienced in the first place (or *what* arises—gross phenomena, subtle phenomena, causal phenomena, or nondual phenomena); and structures and their Views determine *how* these phenomena are experienced and interpreted. The same phenomenon, seen through a different View, will result in a virtually different phenomenon.

For example, let's say a person is in a dream state. This is a subset of the subtle realm, and the subtle is a realm of wild creativity, largely free of the determining constraints and limitations of the gross physical realm, so a person can dream of everything from a unicorn to an important new application of an existing technology. But how a person interprets the dream will depend in large measure on his or her View (or level of structure-rung development). Let's say the person is a Christian, and has a dream of a radiantly luminous being of light and love. They might likely see this being as Jesus Christ himself. If the person is at the conceptual/intentional mind—the egocentric and power-driven mind—because the Magic-Mythic View here is indeed egocentric or capable only of a $1^{st}$-person perspective, the person might see himself—and only himself—as actually being Jesus Christ. If we move up a stage—to the Mythic traditional View, which can adopt a $2^{nd}$-person perspective and thus expand his or her identity from "I" to "we" or "us," and who believes items such as the Bible is the literal word of God; true believers are "the chosen people" (while all others will burn in hell); the miracles in the Bible are all literally true (from Moses parting the Red Sea to Noah and his ark saving all living beings to Christ being born from a biological virgin)—this person might see this being of light that is Jesus Christ as the savior of all true believers; he is the savior of the chosen people (while all those who do not accept him as their personal savior are bound for everlasting hell). At the next higher View—that of the Rational or objective mind—the individual can adopt a $3^{rd}$-person, critical, and reflective attitude—examining the Bible for alleged truths that made sense 2,000 years ago but just don't make sense today (e.g., not eating pork, not speaking to menstruating women, and so on). When Thomas Jefferson sat on the steps of the White House and, with a pair of scissors, began to cut out all portions of the Bible he felt were mythic nonsense, he was expressing a rational point of view. A person at this stage would likely experience this Jesus figure not as the literal sole son of God born from a biological virgin, but rather as a renowned world teacher of great love and wisdom who still has important things to say to the modern world.

The same phenomenon—a being of radiant light—and yet 3 completely different interpretations and experiences of that phenomenon, depending on the subject's structure-stage or View. Now imagine meditation reaching a particular stage of illumination and insight—say, a subtle/luminosity state-stage. The subtle realm and its Vantage Point will determine what types of phenomena can arise in the first place—in this case, luminosity and insight-awareness into impermanence and selflessness—just like the dream subtle realm determined the being of light and feelings of love. But beyond that, in meditation, imagine the difference in actual experience and understanding of a Magic-Mythic View individual (egocentric), a Mythic-Literal View individual (ethnocentric), and a Rational View individual (worldcentric). At that particular point in meditation, the meditation tradition focuses on the particular state-stage itself and the Vantage Point of that stage, which, in deep features, is essentially the same for all 3 of them—luminosity and insight. But the actual texture, the specific nature, the extent, the detailed interpretation, and the perspective will differ in many significant ways between these 3 individuals, depending in large part on their actual View, which in turn depends on the structure-stage and basic rung of the individual's structure center of gravity—seeing that meditation stage from a 1st-person perspective, from a 2nd-person perspective, and from a 3rd-person perspective is to see it very differently in many, many ways. As we've seen, the Vantage Point is one of the important items that determines *what* we see; but View is one of the most important items for *how* we see, the very lens through which we look at this and every experience—how we frame it, how we experience it, how we interpret it, the meaning we give it.

The point is that individuals are already going through meditation practice from different structure-rungs of development, with different Views—not to mention entire schools of Buddhism that are coming from different Views (as we'll see)—and taking both structures and states into account can only have beneficial results in numerous ways. Otherwise, in many cases, if the teacher is at, say, a Pluralistic View, and is interpreting each stage of meditation from a Pluralistic View, then individuals at different Views will have their meditation experience interpreted in ways that often make little sense to them. Often their experience of a particular meditative state-stage will actually be correct for the particular structure-rung they are at, but the meditation teacher will announce it is being incorrectly seen and understood, when in fact it could be being experienced from an even higher structure than the teacher has—say, an Integral or Super-Integral stage. This will severely damage the student's spiritual development, and profoundly misinterpret the higher reaches of Buddhism itself. This happens much more often than is realized. (And—as we'll explore later—it is particularly common with many Eastern teachers, who arrive with a very highly developed state axis—causal or nondual— but a rather poorly developed structure axis, often reflecting the Mythic structure View of the culture they just came from. And when they interact with their students, the majority of whom are often from the higher structure of the Pluralistic View, the results are often severely confusing. The teachers' advice when it comes to states is often brilliant; their advice when it comes from their structure View is often embarrassing, being homophobic, xenophobic, patriarchal, sexist, highly authoritarian, and rigidly hierarchical. Until both structures and states are taken into account, students will be left in these types of utterly confusing situations, and spiritual development itself will often be dysfunctional.)

## STRUCTURES AND VIEWS

We've given several brief summaries of the general state-stages of meditation and contemplation, East and West—gross, subtle, causal, Witnessing, nondual Unity. It remains to give a brief summary of the basic rungs or structures and the structure-stages or Views of development, especially as it impacts religion or spirituality.

First, a brief note on the two major types of spiritual awareness available to humans—that based on structures (also known as *spiritual intelligence*) and that based on states (also known as *spiritual experience*). Spiritual experience, or 1st-person states, is what we have been discussing in terms of meditation and its major state-stages. These are important, we said, because it's how we WAKE UP—how we have direct and immediate experience of the Divine dimensions of Reality—whether nature mysticism of the gross realm, deity mysticism of the subtle realm, formless mysticism of the causal realm, or ultimate unity mysticism of the nondual realm. These are direct, immediate experiences of the Divine Ground of Being as it appears in the various states/realms—gross to subtle to causal to nondual.

Spiritual intelligence, on the other hand, is less experiential and more intellectual or intelligence-oriented (it is, in fact, one of the multiple intelligences). It is oriented to the values and meanings of the Divine Life. From the ideas of Paul Tillich to those of James Fowler, spiritual intelligence is how people have answered the question "What is it that is of ultimate concern to me?"

For someone at rung 1, archaic, it's food and survival. For someone at rung 2, magic, it's sex and emotional pleasure. For someone at rung 3, magic-mythic, it's power and security. For rung 4, group mythic, it's love and conformist belongingness. For rung 5, rational, it's achievement and excellence. For rung 6, pluralistic, it's sensitivity and caring. For rungs 7 and 8, 2nd tier, it's loving embrace and inclusion. For 3rd tier, it's pure self-transcendence and mystical oneness—working with level after level of increasing wholeness. And remember, a person can be at virtually any of those levels or structures while being at virtually any state or realm—the dual center of gravity—the structure-stage and the state-stage, or View and Vantage Point.

In other words, spiritual intelligence is one of perhaps up to a dozen multiple intelligences that humans possess. These include cognitive intelligence, emotional intelligence, moral intelligence, interpersonal intelligence, musical intelligence, aesthetic intelligence, spiritual intelligence, intrapersonal intelligence, mathematico-logical intelligence, and so on. Even though each of those intelligences—or *lines* of development— is quite different from the others, each of them unfolds through the same basic *levels* of development, or the structure-rungs we gave in figure 3.2. Because these *levels* of development (or levels of consciousness) apply equally to all the various *lines* of development, we often represent them with colors instead of names, since a particular name is usually very limiting, but a given color can apply to every multiple intelligence without favoring any.

Thus, to summarize, each of these multiple intelligences or developmental lines is itself composed of structures of consciousness, and each unfolds in developmental structure-stages, moving through the same basic colored levels of development, which are referred to as any given structure's "altitude" ("altitude" meaning "degree of development"). So the different multiple intelligences or lines of development all move through the same basic levels of development indicated by a colored altitude.

Each of these levels of development altitude is, in Integral Theory, a level of consciousness in something quite similar to the Yogachara view; namely, consciousness itself is not a particular thing, process, or phenomena, but the opening or clearing in which various things, processes, and phenomena appear or manifest. The higher the level of consciousness, the greater the number and types of phenomena that can occur on that rung, with the number becoming greater and greater with each increasing level of development (thus, greater consciousness, greater love, greater moral capacity, greater creativity, greater spiritual inclusiveness, greater expanse of values, greater capacity for emotional intelligence, and so on, all of which have been thoroughly and empirically tested and found true).

These basic levels of development (and their associated colors) are given in figures 3.4 and 3.5, along with over a half-dozen major lines of development (including cognitive intelligence, values intelligence, self-identity, worldviews, spiritual intelligence, and needs). The meditation schematic diagram has been included on the right of figure 3.4 to indicate that virtually any of its state-stages can be experienced by virtually any of the structure-levels in any of the lines. Now, since spiritual intelligence is one of the multiple intelligences or developmental lines—and since it is of direct relevance to our present topic—I'll run through the major stages of spiritual intelligence in a bit more detail—as we ran through some of the major meditative states of spiritual experience—and I'll relate them to Fowler's pioneering work, while using them

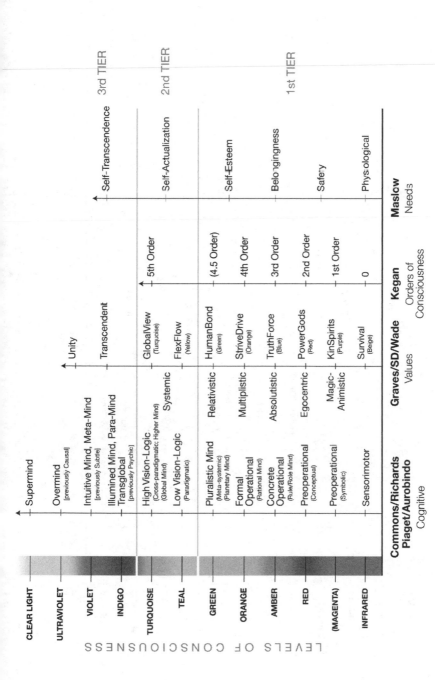

FIGURE 3.4. *Some major developmental lines.*

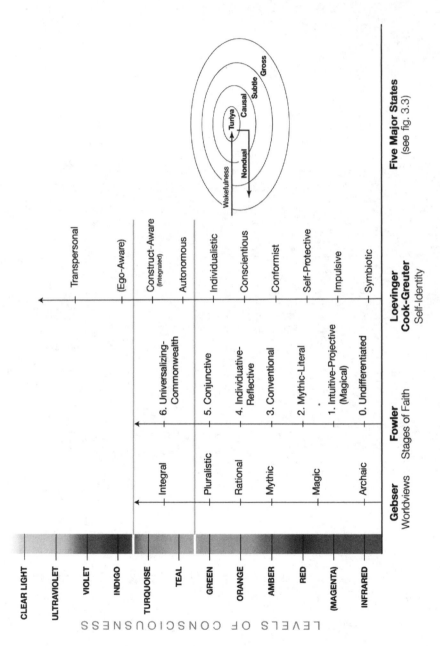

FIGURE 3.5. *Gebser, Fowler, Loevinger/Cook-Greuter.*

to give an indication of some of the general characteristics of each of the major levels of development themselves.

## SPIRITUAL INTELLIGENCE

So here are a few details on the various Views of structure-stages, particularly in relation to the spiritual intelligence View. Much of this is in sync with James Fowler's monumentally pioneering work, *Stages of Faith*. Humankind has known, for hundreds, even thousands, of years that spirituality or religious orientation depends on states of consciousness and state-stages. But Fowler was one of the first to show, with substantial evidence and research, that a person's spiritual orientation also depends on structure-stages of development. These, of course, were variations on the standard, general levels of development—whose Views we have been calling archaic, magic, mythic, rational, pluralistic, and integral. But his actual research and realms of data relating specifically to spiritual development were what made his efforts so pioneering. After giving a few details from some of the more important structure-stages, I'll give specific examples of Buddhism at each stage.

The *Magic* View, or magenta structure-stage, Fowler called "intuitive-projective." It's focused on safety, security, and survival, and magical charms to both secure survival and ward off evil spirits. It's very anthropomorphic and superstitious. Fantasy thinking is common; such thinking equates and confuses wholes and parts; and equates all wholes with similar parts (the basis of prejudice—e.g., if one black-skinned person is dangerous, all black-skinned people are dangerous). The image of an object is not clearly differentiated from the real object (e.g., stick a pin in a toy doll representing a person and something bad will happen to the real person). Ancestor worship starts to become common, and is often the source of petitionary prayers. Tales and legends are a common source of community bonding. The basic rung at the Magic View (impulsive, fantasy, emotional-sexual) is limited to a 1st-person perspective, so the individual is more concerned with his own salvation than that of others.

The *Magic-Mythic* View, or red structure-stage, Fowler calls "mythic-literal." The difference between magic and mythic is where the source of "miracle power" is located. In magic, it is the self—I do a rain dance, and Nature obediently rains. In mythic, the self has surrendered the illusion that it can miraculously intervene in nature and history and change it; but if it can no longer perform miracles, God can (or Goddess or some other supernatural being). This magic-mythic stage marks the transition from a previously omnipotent and magic self to an omnipotent and magic God or Gods (themselves mythic; hence, magic-mythic)—a stage Spiral Dynamics calls "PowerGods." There is a concomitant emphasis on, and belief in, miracles. I can't do them, but God can, and if I ritualistically approach God in a way that pleases Him, then He (or She) will perform a miracle for me. Mythic narratives begin to develop, and magical incantations are believed to put one in right relationship to Divinity, which will then more likely intervene in nature and history on your behalf. The basic rung supporting this View—the conceptual, representational, vital mind—is still largely limited to a 1st-person perspective, and so narcissistic power is a major concern (both in oneself and in Divinity—"PowerGods"). God is powerful, wrathful, vengeful. Still superstitious, self-centered, animistically infused.

The *Mythic* View, or amber structure-stage, Fowler calls "synthetic-conventional," "conventional" because the basic structure-rung can take the role of other—can adopt a 2nd-person perspective—and hence one's View switches from egocentric to ethnocentric, and one's identity expands from the individual self to the group—the clan, the tribe, the religion, community, nation. One's morality likewise shifts from egocentric to strongly conformist—"my county, right or wrong; my religion, right or wrong; my group, right or wrong." Strong boundaries are drawn between "Us" and "Them," and religiously, my group is God's "chosen people." My life becomes devoted to jihad, by whatever name, or the desire to either convert or kill nonbelievers. Killing nonbelievers is not a sin; it's a promotion, a religious promotion. There is a strong desire to understand God's truth, which is often believed to be contained in one book (the Bible, Koran, Pure Land Sutra, Mao's Little Red Book), which is often a mythic narrative taken to be absolutely and literally true (Elijah really did ascend into Heaven in a chariot while still alive; God really did rain locusts on the Egyptians and kill all of their firstborn males; Lao Tzu really was 900 years old when he was born, and so on). Those who believe in God's word are destined for Heaven, those who don't, everlasting hellfire. The concrete operational or rule/role mind supporting this View makes both the rules and one's roles very important, to be rigidly followed. Breaking the rules or violating the roles can lead to damnation (if this stage is institutionalized, excommunication). Rigid social hierarchies, and religious hierarchies, are common, such as the caste system or the Church. For those within a chosen group, love and compassion are recommended, since these are all God's chosen children. For those outside the group, conversion, torture, or murder are a few of the options. For more moderate believers, charity and good works are common, since the implicit belief is that the recipients are at least potential converts to the chosen group.

The *Modern-Rational* View, or orange structure-stage, Fowler calls "individuative-reflective," "reflective" because the basic rung of formal operational has added a 3rd-person perspective, from which an individual can take up a more reflective, objective, critical, even skeptical view of his or her experiences and beliefs. "Rational," as the general name of this View, doesn't mean dry, abstract, distanced, viciously analytical, or such. Rather, it means it can understand conditional worlds—"what if" and "as if"—and thus begin not only to question the literal truth of mythic religious beliefs, but instead to read them with more symbolic and metaphoric meanings. Beliefs tend to be based on evidence and universal reasonableness. All individuals are treated fairly, regardless of race, color, sex, or creed. In terms of spiritual intelligence, an atheistic, an agnostic, and a religious believer can all be at the Rational level, as long as they have reached their conclusions through logic, evidence, and reflexive considerations, including the perfectly logical conclusion that logic alone is not necessarily the only form of knowledge, and other, more intuitive modes deserve equal consideration. Again, when Thomas Jefferson sat on the White House steps and furiously cut up his Bible with a pair of scissors, he was leaving those sections that passed these tests and rejecting the others. When Bishop Shelby Spong, a well-known Christian theologian, does essentially the same thing with his Bible, he's subjecting his religious beliefs to those based less on child-like myths and more on reason and evidence, and still coming out the other side a strong and devoted believer in the essentials of the Christian faith, as seen through the Rational and Pluralistic Views. Buddhism, from the start, has been at least a Rational View, based not on dogma, authority, or mere faith—and containing little if any mythological gods and goddesses—but based instead directly on one's own experience and reason (although not all followers lived up to those levels, as we'll see).

The *Postmodern-Pluralist* View, or green structure-stage, Fowler calls "conjunctive." Supported by the basic structure-rung of the pluralistic mind, it is devoted to taking as many perspectives as possible (an endeavor that reaches a real fruition at the next stage, the holistic-integral). Combined with the fact that it is but a step away from the genuine holism of 2$^{nd}$ tier, this View is deeply interested in wholeness, reconciliation, and nonmarginalizing. There's not just a passive tolerance of other religions, but often an active embrace. This View doesn't just abide other Views, but often actually seeks to understand them and incorporate them into its own worldview. (It is ultimately hampered in this approach by the fact that it is still 1$^{st}$ tier, and so still believes that this pluralistic stance itself is the one and only true stance there is, which itself is a contradiction postmodernism has never managed to navigate adequately, believing its view is superior in a world where nothing is supposed to be superior.) But with this "almost Integral" or "half Integral" stance, if you will, the Pluralistic View sees important truths in all religions, even if it feels most comfortable in its own, and often seeks to incorporate aspects of other religions into its own. It deconstructs traditional hierarchies; speaks out strongly for the oppressed and disadvantaged; has a strongly planetary and environmental sensibility; is particularly open to nature mysticism and spirit in 3$^{rd}$ person as the Great Web of Life and the Universe Story. It is socially engaged, actively supports minority rights, and advocates for sustainability in all walks of life. This is a relatively new View, with its supporting basic structure of the pluralistic mind having itself evolved in any significant degree only beginning during the student revolutions of the '6os, themselves driven largely by this stage. A person at this level of spiritual intelligence can be theistic, nontheistic, atheistic, agnostic, or odd combinations thereof, as long as they are conclusions reached by this altitude of development.

One of its most notable characteristics is its denial and condemnation of every form of hierarchy. In this, it fails to distinguish between dominator hierarchies (which are indeed loathsome) and actualization hierarchies (which are the form of most growth processes in nature, including humans). In dominator hierarchies, with each higher level, the few dominate and oppress the many. In growth hierarchies, each higher level is more and more inclusive. For example, a central growth hierarchy in nature is atoms to molecules to cells to organisms. In that hierarchy, each higher level literally includes and embraces the junior—it doesn't oppress it (molecules don't oppress atoms—if anything they love and embrace them). The most commonly used evidence to condemn all hierarchy is Carol Gilligan's book *In a Different Voice*, where she argues that men and women think differently— men emphasize rights, justice, autonomy, and hierarchy, and women think more in terms of relationship, care, communion, and nonhierarchy. Many feminists assumed that since most rottenness in the world is patriarchal, and since dominator hierarchies are bad, and all men think hierarchically, then all hierarchies are bad.

But Gilligan makes a second point in her book, a point studiously overlooked. Although men may think hierarchically and women nonhierarchically, both men and women develop through the same 4 hierarchical stages. In women, Gilligan called these stages selfish (egocentric), care (where concern expands from self to group, or ethnocentric), universal care (all peoples, or worldcentric), and integrated (where both men and women integrate the contra-sexual mode). In other words, women's nonhierarchical thinking develops through 4 hierarchical stages—in other words, a growth hierarchy. In cutting out all hierarchies, feminists cut out all women's growth. An unfortunate move, to put it mildly.

But that's what the Pluralistic View does—it cuts out all hierarchies, or flattens them, as the current phrase has it. And thus in heroically deconstructing all dominator hierarchies, postmodernism catastrophically deconstructs and destroys all growth hierarchies as well, a cultural and spiritual catastrophe. But the denial of all hierarchies or ranking is one of the surest indicators you're dealing with the pluralistic level of development.

The next stage—the *Integral* View (teal and turquoise altitude)—what Fowler calls "universalizing"—puts us right at the very edge of today's evolution, at least as far as structures are concerned. Although rare Integral pioneers can be spotted a thousand years ago, or more, 2nd tier only reached more than 1% of the population in the 1970s and more than 5% at the turn of the millennium, only a decade or so ago. Wherever it appears, there is a concomitant drive to find patterns that connect, the unities under the diversities, the wholeness that goes with every partness, the oneness alongside every manyness. The emergence of the Integral mode— even at today's 5%, let alone at the prophesized soon-to-be 10%—is a monumental turning point in evolution itself, whose impact simply cannot be overemphasized.

Recall some of the characteristics of the Integral stages— rungs 7 and 8, supported by low and high vision-logic (or teal and turquoise)—which cognize wholes, connections, and unity-in-diversities. First and foremost, it's $2^{nd}$ tier; unlike each $1^{st}$-tier View that believes its truths and values are the only real truths and values in existence, $2^{nd}$ tier sees important contributions made by all previous stages, rungs, and Views. If nothing else, each junior level becomes a component or subholon in each succeeding senior level, as each stage of evolution transcends and includes its predecessor. A whole proton becomes part of an atom; a whole atom becomes part of a molecule; a whole molecule becomes part of a cell; a whole cell becomes part of a whole organism. Each stage is a whole/part, or holon, and the resultant nested hierarchy is a growth holarchy. The Integral stages intuit this, and thus see the importance of every preceding stage of development, not just in humans, but in the Kosmos at large, going all the way back to the Big Bang. The Integral View sees itself as intrinsically interwoven with the entire universe—this is an interconnected, seamless, vital, living, creative, and conscious Kosmos, and the same evolutionary drive to higher and higher wholes is the same force that produced mammals from dust and Integral from Archaic—a fundamental, intrinsic drive of the Kosmos that Whitehead called "the creative advance into novelty" (and Integral Theory calls "Eros"). Integral levels are creative and highly conscious; each moment is new, fresh, spontaneous, and alive. It is the first stage to integrate knowing and feeling, consciousness and being, epistemology and ontology, and not fracture them from each other and then try to "ground" one in the other, but rather seeing and feeling them to be complementary aspects of the seamless Whole of Reality, operating not by disembodied reflection or representation but by embodied mutual resonance within all 4 quadrants.

Thus, unlike the previous Pluralistic View, the Integral View is truly holistic, not in any New Age woo-woo sense but as being evidence of a deeply interwoven and interconnected and conscious Kosmos. The Pluralistic View, we saw, wants to be holistic and all-inclusive and nonmarginalizing, but it loathes the modern Rational View, absolutely cannot abide the traditional Mythic View, goes apoplectic when faced with a truly Integral View. But the Integral stages are truly and genuinely inclusive. First, all of the previous structure-rungs are literally included as components of the Integral structure-rung, or vision-logic, a fact that is intuited at this stage. Views, of course, are negated, and so somebody at an Integral View is not including directly a Magic View, a Mythic View, a Rational View, and so on. By definition, that is impossible. A View is generated when the central self *exclusively* identifies with a particular rung of development. Somebody at a Rational View is exclusively identified with the corresponding rung at that stage—namely, formal operational. To have access directly to, say, a Magic View—which means the View of the world when *exclusively identified* with the impulsive or emotional-sexual rung—the individual would have to give up Rationality, give up the concrete mind, give up the representational mind, give up language itself, and regress totally to the impulsive mind (something that won't happen without severe brain damage). The Rational person still has complete access to the emotional-sexual *rung*, but not the exclusive *View* from that rung. As we saw, rungs are included, Views are negated. (Just like on a real ladder—if you're at, say, the 7th rung in the ladder, all previous 6 rungs are still present and still in existence, holding up the 7th rung; but, while you are standing on the 7th rung, you can't directly see what the world looks like from those earlier rungs. Those were gone when you stepped off those rungs onto higher ones, and so at this point you have all the rungs, but only the View from the highest rung you're on, in this case, the 7th-rung View.) So a person at Integral doesn't directly, in their own makeup, have immediate access to earlier Views (archaic, magic, mythic, and so on), but they do have access to all the earlier corresponding rungs (sensorimotor, emotional-sexual, conceptual, rule/role, and so on), and thus they can generally intuit what rung a particular person's center of gravity is at, and thus indirectly be able to understand what View or worldview that person is expressing (magic, mythic, rational, pluralistic, and so on). And by "include those worldviews" what is meant is that the Integral levels actively tolerate and make room for those Views in their own holistic outreach. They might not agree fully with them (they don't do so in their own makeup, having transcended and negated junior Views), but they intuitively understand the significance and importance of all Views in the unfolding sweep of evolutionary development. Further, they understand that a person has the right to stop growing at virtually any View, and thus each particular View will become, for some people, an actual station in Life, and their values, needs, and motivations will be expressions of that particular View in Life. And thus a truly enlightened, inclusive society will make some sort of room for traditional values, modern values, postmodern values, and so on. Everybody is born at square one and thus begins their development of Views at the lowest rung and continues from there, so every society will consist of a different mix of percentages of people at different altitude rungs and Views of the overall spectrum. In most Western countries, for example—and this varies depending on exactly how you measure it—but generally, about 10% of the population is at Magic, 40% at traditional Mythic, 40%–50% at modern Rational, 20% at postmodern Pluralistic, 5% at Holistic/Integral, and less than 1% at Super-Integral. (This doesn't add up exactly to 100%, because there is some overlap.)

And yet only an Integral View has that understanding of inclusiveness, which means, as evolution continues to move into Integral levels, society is poised for perhaps the most momentous transformation in its entire history—into a genuinely *inclusive* society. And there's been nothing like it before because there has never been a major *tier* transformation before. All previous transformations were stage transformations. But the transformation from the green Pluralistic stage to the teal/turquoise Integral stage is, in addition to being a stage transformation, also and simultaneously a transformation from 1st tier to 2nd tier—and that, *that*, is epic, revolutionary, and utterly unprecedented. We don't even have any examples of how to construct a radically inclusive, all-rung, all-View society, where all Views are given a voice, perhaps differently weighted, but a voice nonetheless, as each stage of development becomes a welcome station in Life.

As far as spirituality and spiritual intelligence go, an Integral spiritual intelligence doesn't mean that all religions will be melted down into one, single, universal religion (any more than the international style of cooking means all food becomes Italian). It does mean, however, that individuals at the Integral stages of spiritual intelligence will demand Integral versions of their own faith. There are several somewhat different models of Integral—these stages of development, remember, aren't marked by their specific contents but by the degree of complexity of thinking and the degree of consciousness available (or the number of perspectives inherent at that level—archaic through magic-mythic are 1st-person perspectives; mythic adds a 2nd-person perspective; rational adds 3rd-person; pluralistic, 4th-person; holistic and integral, 5th- and 6th-person; super-integral, 7th-person and higher)—and the point is that, within those degrees of complexity and consciousness, many different models are possible. But all of them, if truly Integral, will want to include the essentials of the others, and so these models tend to converge. That's what the Integral AQAL model—referring to all quadrants, all levels (all lines, all states, all types)—attempts to do, and using that model as a framework, virtually any Integral Spirituality—whether Christian, Buddhist, Muslim, Hindu, Jewish, and so on—will likely include several elements, either as found in their own traditions or, if necessary, imported from other traditions and human disciplines, including the sciences.

We'll summarize these new elements of a possible Fourth Turning, or Integral Spirituality/Integral Buddhism, in the next chapter.

# 4

## AN EXAMPLE OF A MORE INTEGRAL SPIRITUALITY

S O, WHAT MIGHT BE added to the already existing spiritual
frameworks to bring them up to date; to make them more
inclusive, more integral; to bring Buddhism into a Fourth
Great Turning of the Wheel of Spiritual Truth or Dharma; to
make spirituality compatible with the modern and postmodern world, and not just an embarrassment to it? Immanuel
Kant said you can tell this is a modern world because if you
walked into a room and found someone praying, they would
be embarrassed. What kind of spirituality would *not* be embarrassing? Here are a few of the dozen of possible additions
that I believe are the most crucial:

### RUNGS AND VIEWS

1. To start with, *structures and structure-stages of development*—or rungs and Views. Any Integral Spirituality would
include its fundamental tenets as interpreted in the language
of each of the major Views. There would be a Magic teaching, a Magic-Mythic teaching, a Mythic teaching, a Rational

teaching, a Pluralistic teaching, an Integral teaching, and a Super-Integral teaching. The point, for any overall faith, is to start early childhood with a Magical teaching—where a hero (a saint, sage, or adept) of the tradition is treated as a superman or superhero, much like any superhero of any children's Saturday morning cartoon show, which reflects the Magic view perfectly—they can fly, walk on water, see through walls, raise the dead. (This is not to send the message that, in adulthood, this religion will make you Superman, only that the practice of religion brings many powerful benefits, and will help you with many of Life's most difficult problems.)

As the child grows into early school years, Magic teaching gives way to Magic-Mythic, or "PowerGods," still reflecting the essentially egocentric nature of thinking, with the added drive and allure of newly emergent power-drives, but also shifting the source of "miraculous" occasions from the self to powerful others, opening the dimension of Spirit as a Great Thou, but also teaching there is Good Help and Advice from knowledgeable Others—from adepts, teachers, and sages from the tradition.

As a child enters later school years and early adolescence, Magic-Mythic switches to Mythic, which, with its group-and-conformist orientation, fits the rule/role mind and peer pressure so characteristic of this period. Late adolescence and early adulthood brings the crucial transformation from ethnocentric Mythic to worldcentric Rational, perhaps the most important transformation prior to 2$^{nd}$ tier. The emphasis here is on showing that using reason and evidence, there is abundant support for a spiritual dimension to the Kosmos, especially if one includes meditation. (Reasons for a spiritual dimension include humanity's own highest states of consciousness, which uniformly disclose an ultimate Reality sewn into the very fabric of the universe; the "creative advance into novelty" demonstrated by evolution itself; the evidence from numerous sciences on the interwoven, entangled, enacted, interconnected nature of all seemingly separate things and events; the presence of consciousness as an undeniable reality throughout the universe; and most significantly, the experimental and injunctive proof of Spirit's existence by following paradigms, practices, and exemplars, from contemplation to highest yoga—this is not God taken on faith but based on direct personal experience.) A significant characteristic of the Rational View, which is what makes it so important for today's world, is the introduction of a $3^{rd}$-person perspective, which moves the religion from an *ethnocentric* "us versus them" to a *worldcentric* "all of us," where all humans are treated the same, regardless of race, color, sex, or creed. A major aim of the Rational stage of spiritual intelligence is to demythologize the tradition, cleaning it of magic and mythic elements characteristic of the childhood of humanity, a childhood experienced not only today but several thousand years ago when many of the world's major religions themselves were being laid down. Spirit has continued to evolve, and so should spirituality.

If development continues, then in young adulthood, the Rational View appropriately gives way to the Pluralistic View, as continuing life experiences show that there are often many more and different perspectives on an issue than monolithic rationality lets on—that "there are more things in heaven and earth than are dreamt of in your philosophy." The Pluralistic stage also acts to make sure the particular faith is trying to be inclusive, socially engaged, sustainable, nonoppressive, and environmentally sound. Pluralistic-View spirituality is politically sensitive (usually liberal), actively tolerant (though it still dislikes other value systems—Mythic, Rational, Integral, and so on). It is interested in everything "conscious," from conscious capitalism to conscious aging to conscious parenting; feminist, womanist, and more recently, masculinist; and relationship-oriented ("The new Buddha will be the Sangha"). Again, it's important to remember that someone at the Pluralist-View stage of spiritual intelligence may be totally atheist, or theist, or nontheist, or agnostic, as long as he or she reached their conclusions with a pluralistic mind and a 4$^{th}$-person perspective.

Now it is possible to introduce simplified Integral models and maps as early as high school (and there is much to recommend doing so), but when development is left to its own devices, Integral stages tend to emerge in early midlife. The major reason is simply time. Robert Kegan, noted Harvard developmentalist, estimates that, on average, it takes about 5 years to move through any major level of development. Integral stages, which emerge roughly at the 7$^{th}$ major developmental level, would thus come in at 35 years old, generally. As more and more individuals move into Integral, we find more and more developing early or proto-Integral Views in late high school and early college. Be that as it may, the Integral-View spiritual stance has the major characteristics I'm briefly outlining. It might not want to literally include all other religions, but it wants its own religion to be all-inclusive, including the items I'm listing now, starting with rungs and Views. Integral Spirituality understands that individuals grow and develop through various stages, and this includes their View and understanding of spirituality. Spiritual teachings themselves should therefore be adapted and presented in the appropriate language and level of difficulty for each stage—magic to mythic to rational to pluralistic to integral to super-integral.

Other items that an Integral Spirituality would include (which I'll outline in a moment) include states of consciousness (and state-stages, or Vantage Points); the dual center of gravity of overall development (View and Vantage Point); quadrants (or the 1-2-3 of Spirit, explained below); major typologies (such as the Enneagram); and shadow and shadow work. An Integral Spirituality recognizes that human beings have several different but equally important dimensions to their makeup—such as their major perspective orientation (or quadrant), their major level of development in general (or structure center of gravity), their major state center of gravity, their major personality type, and various unconscious, or shadow, elements—and that Spirit operates in and through all of those. Failing to take any of those dimensions into account—at least in a simplified or introductory fashion—is to catastrophically ignore and deny that dimension of Spirit. It is to approach the world spiritually blind in many of our eyes. It is to stumble numbed and crippled into the universe, hobbled in some of the most important ways God tries to reach us, touch us, speak to us, Awaken us. An Integral Spirituality demands we spiritually approach matter, body, mind, soul, and Spirit in self, culture, and nature—nothing less.

Finally, in terms of overall spiritual intelligence—which we have been briefly tracking—on the other side of the leading edge of evolution we have 3 or 4 higher, at this point mostly potential, levels of development, including levels of spiritual intelligence. Individually, their basic structure-rungs are referred to as para-mind, meta-mind, overmind, and supermind; collectively, they are called 3rd tier. What all 3rd-tier structures have in common is some degree of direct transpersonal identity and experience. Further, each 3rd-tier structure of consciousness is integrated, in some fashion, with a particular state of consciousness (often, para-mental with the gross, meta-mental with subtle, overmind with causal/Witnessing, and supermind with nondual, although this varies with each individual's actual history). Previously, in 1ˢᵗ and 2ⁿᵈ tier, structures and states were relatively independent. One could have a state center of gravity at gross and yet structurally evolve all the way to Integral without fully objectifying the gross state (i.e., fully making it an object, fully transcending it). But beginning with the 3ʳᵈ-tier para-mind, whenever you experience that structure, you also implicitly or intuitively understand or experience the gross realm as objectified, which means that state is intimately connected to the structure at this level, which gives rise, or can give rise, to expanded states such as nature mysticism (this can be experienced at earlier levels but not inherently, and is interpreted according to the Views of those lower levels; but at this level becomes an inherent potential). Likewise, because of the conjunction with the gross state, this level often carries variations of the realization that the physical world is not merely physical, but is rather psychophysical in its true nature. This can also evoke flashes of higher state presences, such as Witnessing states or even nondual. And so on with the subtle state and meta-mind; causal/Witnessing and overmind; and nondual Suchness and supermind. Those states are all "minimally" connected to those structures, in the sense that, for example, a person at meta-mind might have already and previously moved his or her state center of gravity to subtle, but if not, the person cannot proceed beyond the meta-mind without doing so at this point. And likewise with causal/Witnessing and overmind; and nondual Suchness and supermind.

The difference between supermind and Big Mind (if we take Big Mind to mean the state experience of nondual Suchness, or turiyatita) is that Big Mind can be experienced or recognized at virtually any lower level or rung, Magic to Integral. In fact, one can be at, say, the Pluralistic stage, and experience several core characteristics of the entire sequence of state-stages (gross to subtle to causal to Witnessing to Non-dual), although, of course, the entire sequence, including non-dual Suchness, will be interpreted in Pluralistic terms. This is unfortunate in many ways—interpreting Dharma in merely Pluralistic terms (or Mythic terms, or Rational, and so on)—because it is so ultimately reductionistic; but it happens all the time, given the relative independence of states and structures at $1^{st}$ and $2^{nd}$ tier.

Supermind, on the other hand, as a basic structure-rung (conjoined with nondual Suchness) can only be experienced once all the previous junior levels have emerged and developed, and as in all structure development, stages cannot be skipped. Therefore, unlike Big Mind, supermind can only be experienced after all $1^{st}$-, $2^{nd}$-, and $3^{rd}$-tier junior stages have been passed through. While, as Genpo Roshi has abundantly demonstrated, Big Mind state experience is available to virtually anybody at almost any age (and will be interpreted according to the View of their current stage), supermind is an extremely rare recognition. Supermind, as the highest structure-rung to date, has access to all previous structures, all the way back to Archaic—and the Archaic itself, of course, has transcended and included, and now embraces, every major structural evolution going all the way back to the Big Bang. (A human being literally enfolds and embraces all the major transformative unfoldings of the entire Kosmic history—strings to quarks to subatomic particles to atoms to molecules to cells, all the way through the Tree of Life up to its latest evolutionary emergent, the triune brain, the most complex structure in the known natural world.) Supermind, in any given individual, is experienced as a type of "omniscience"—the supermind, since it transcends and includes *all* of the previous structure-rungs, and inherently is conjoined with the highest nondual Suchness state, has a full and complete knowledge of all of the potentials in that person. It literally "knows all," at least for that individual.

A Super-Integral Spirituality has all the features of an Integral Spirituality, plus, among other things, an inherent conjunction of each stage with a given state, giving all of its stages a transpersonal or spiritual flavor (at least the possibility of either gross nature mysticism, subtle deity mysticism, causal formless mysticism, or nondual Unity mysticism). These mystical states are, of course, available to virtually all the lower $1^{st}$- and $2^{nd}$-tier stages, although there are likely some significant differences in $3^{rd}$ tier, given its inherent conjunction of structures and states.

The whole point of understanding the different forms spirituality takes at each major View of development is to create, in each tradition, *a conveyor belt of spiritual teaching and practice*—with different forms of teaching and practice at magic, magic-mythic, mythic, rational, pluralistic, holistic, and integral (and super-integral increasingly common in the future). This conveyor belt would pick an individual up in his or her early years, and transform with them—and help them transform—at each succeeding rung and View (helping them move from magic to mythic to rational to pluralistic to integral to super-integral). As it is now, most religions are stuck at some form of mythic View, while the other intelligences are free to move into rational, pluralistic, holistic, and integral Views (occasionally higher). This spiritually arrested development is a cultural catastrophe of the first magnitude. Spiritual intelligence is the only multiple intelligence that evolved to interact with ultimate reality and ultimate truth and ultimate goodness. All other intelligences interact only with relative truth; spiritual intelligence interacts with absolute truth. It ought to be leading the other intelligences by a stage or two, acting as a guiding beacon for all of them. As it is, stuck at mythic, it generally lags a stage or two behind most other intelligences, so that our growth and evolution is being hampered by our very View of Spirit itself, an infinitely heavy lead albatross hanging around our developmental necks. God itself is slowing our evolution (when in reality, God is creating it!). No wonder it's so easy for the "new atheists" to make so much fun of religion. In its typical mythic-literal form, for adults it's indeed laughable (although perfectly appropriate for a school-age child, as we saw).

Structures and their Views are one of the first and most important items that any truly new and inclusive spirituality would want to include. Structures are the very tools with which the mind sees, experiences, and interprets the world—including spiritual state and meditative experiences—and structures, like virtually all components of the mind (and nature) show development. An infant is simply not born with full access to logic, rationality, vision-logic, the para-mind, or any tools, capacities, functions, and structures higher than Archaic. As these various higher capacities emerge, they do so in qualitatively distinct stages or structures or levels or waves of development, co-creating a different world (and different needs, motivations, worldviews, capacity for love and care and tolerance, moral maturity, aesthetic richness, sense of self-identity, and a dozen other capacities) at each structure-stage. Structures are a recent discovery of humankind, being barely a hundred years old—discovered much too late to be included in the great spiritual systems, most of which are a thousand years or older. But since structures determine how we experience and interpret our world—including our spiritual understanding and experience—they have a direct hand to play in how spiritual understanding and experience is interpreted at each and every stage of mental-tool-making, interpretive-capacity-generating, structure or basic rung development. There is, it's not too strong to say, a different God, a different Spirit, seen and experienced and understood at each and every one of these major rungs—different stage, different God (or different dharma, dogma, gospel, spiritual truth). Each of them is perfectly adequate for the stage and capacities of the rung at which it emerges—and putting them all together gives us a spectrum or (in a more graphic level-crunching metaphor) a conveyor belt of significantly different Spirit after Spirit after Spirit, until we reach the very upper limits of Spirit's own evolution at this point in history and overall human development (always understanding that yet-higher Spiritual unfoldings are not only possible but likely).

But the upper limit of spiritual development at any point in history and evolution includes the sum total of all structures and all states that have emerged at that point in time. This realizes that a fully mature spirituality is not only one where we have largely experienced a complete Enlightenment or WAKING UP in our *state* development, but that such an Enlightenment is experienced, not in childish or adolescent ways or Views, but in a profoundly GROWN UP fashion or View, significantly matured into the wiser, more-perspective-containing, more inclusive and tolerant and integral structures that have recently emerged and been discovered by humankind. This new version of Enlightenment (or full development) of both of our dual centers of gravity (structure View and state Vantage Point) becomes a new bar for the measurement of human growth, development, and evolution.

In this regard I would mention the works of one of my very brightest students, Dustin DiPerna, although he is also an original and creative theorist in his own right. In 2 volumes— *Streams of Wisdom: An Advanced Guide to Integral Spiritual Development* and *Evolution's Alley: Our World's Religious Traditions as Conveyor Belts of Evolution*—he sets out to supply extra evidence to some of the key tenets of Integral Spirituality, including the 4 major vectors of development (structures and structure-stages or Views, states and state-stages or Vantage Points). He uses Magic, Mythic, Rational, Pluralistic, and Integral Views; gross, subtle, causal, Witnessing, and Nondual state-realms and their Vantage Points; and gives examples of all 5 stages of Views in Christianity, Islam, Hinduism, and Buddhism.

Since we're looking at a possible Fourth Turning in Buddhism, I'll focus on his examples here, and add a few of my own. The point is that there are *already* major schools of Buddhism at every one of the major Views of structure development we have discussed; but they are not realized as being interpretations of Dharma driven by different structure-stages, but are simply taken as different, sometimes warring views over a single View of Buddhadharma. Bringing different structure-rungs and Views into the picture helps clarify enormously something that is *already* happening (but not understood).

Buddhism began as a Rational system, one of the few world religions to do so. And remember how we are using "rational"—it doesn't mean dry, abstract, analytic, and alienated. It means capable of at least a 3$^{rd}$-person perspective; it can therefore introspect and reflect on its own awareness and experience, adopt a critical and self-critical stance, understand "what if" and "as if" worlds, step back from the self and take a detached, nonattached view. The book title *Buddhism: The Rational Religion* says it all. And I think it is this rational core that continues to make Buddhism so appealing to the modern West. As many have pointed out, Buddhism is closer to a psychology than a typical religion. Of course most schools of Buddhism put a central emphasis on states, but when it comes to their interpretation, it is rational, objective, and evidence-based.

Of course, not everybody is born at Rational. Actually, nobody is. All individuals start their development of basic rungs and Views at sensorimotor and Archaic, and move from there to Magic, then Mythic, Rational, Pluralistic, Integral, and Super-Integral (or until development stops). And this means individuals at all of those stages can be attracted to Buddhism, and over the centuries, actual schools of Buddhism have arisen based in each of them.

Melford Spiro in his work *Buddhism and Society* divided Burmese Theravada into three groups, and they are almost exactly equivalent to Magic, Mythic, and Rational. The first, which he calls Apotropaic Buddhism, is primarily concerned with protection from evil spirits, using items such as magical charms and incantations. This is pure Magic. Dustin adds the literal versions of some Pure Land schools, where the single repetition of Buddha's name ensures rebirth in a Pure Land heaven.

Spiro's second group he calls Kammatic Buddhism, which is focused on generating merit for a future rebirth. This is a typically Mythic View with some magic elements. Dustin points to the ethnocentric warfare of the Sinhala Buddhists fighting in Sri Lanka. They possess all of Marty and Appleby's "family resemblances" of mythic-literal fundamentalists—a strong sense of religious identity (a "true believer"), strict social boundaries (us versus them), reliance on myth, and so on. Sinhala Buddhists see themselves as "owners and protectors of the Buddhist teachings"; they view Sri Lanka as the home of the true Dharma; they claim control over the purity and right version of the Dharma; and they are "ethnic chauvinists" in constant warfare (holy war) with Tamil Hindus, the enemy of truth. This is, indeed, almost pure ethnocentric and absolutistic Mythic stage.

Spiro's third group he calls Nibbanic Buddhism—they are interested in attaining Nirvana through state-realization as described by Theravada. This Rational Buddhism (including its emphasis on states) is, as we noted, probably the closest thing we have to Gautama Buddha's original teaching. The Rational nature of Early Buddhism also meant it was not ethnocentric, as Mythic is, but worldcentric (which treats all people not as being a member of an "in group" versus an "out group" but equally, regardless of race, color, sex, or creed). Hence, Early Buddhism opened itself to the untouchables, usually excluded from other religions. This was a major factor in Buddhism's rapid spread through India. Dustin adds D. T. Suzuki, the famous Japanese Zen author who probably did the most to introduce the West to Zen Buddhism. The historian Lynn White said something to the effect that the translation of D. T. Suzuki's *Essays in Zen Buddhism* into English will rank with the translation of the Latin Bible into English. In over a dozen books, Suzuki patiently and rationally explained the nonrational core of Zen, and did so brilliantly.

The Pluralistic View is marked by deep social concern and powerful drives of social justice; is egalitarian and antihierarchical; is seriously concerned with environmental and ecological issues; argues for sustainability and renewable energy; downplays any sort of ranking; is antipatriarchal and antiwar; is profeminist; and is profoundly socially engaged. It is, in other words, the standard form of Buddhism in the Western world. Dustin gives socially engaged Buddhism as a prime example.

As I mentioned earlier, this led to all manner of difficulties with the first wave of Eastern teachers in the 1960s and 1970s. Most of them had come from Mythic cultures and ethnocentric backgrounds; accordingly they were often extremely authoritarian; very hierarchical; often patriarchal, hence sexist; usually xenophobic; often homophobic. They were used to teachers being in positions of unquestioned authority, and acted that way. They were also unaccustomed to acting in the atmosphere of radical sexual openness, freedom, and looseness of their students, who nonetheless expected a radical purity in the teacher (a majority of whom failed conspicuously to meet these standards). These Mythic or at most Rational teachers met students who were largely Pluralistic, and a profound View clash resulted. This was complicated by the fact that the teachers, although often lagging behind their students in structure development and View, were massively more developed than their students when it came to states and state-stages, many being at causal or nondual stages. This caused profound confusion in the students, who couldn't tell if the advice from a teacher was coming from an outmoded Mythic View or a truly advanced-state Vantage Point. "How can he know so much about higher states yet be so homophobic? How can he be so awakened to equalizing Nonduality yet so authoritarian? How can he be so liberated and yet take such advantage of his female students?"

And so the structure/state discrepancies went, causing enormous problems and heartaches on both sides. I know two fully transmitted American Zen Masters who faced a particularly difficult version of this, and finally decided the only way to get through their training was to "swallow the whole fish"—fully accept the retarded structural advice along with the advanced state advice. They have both subsequently surrendered their mantels of orthodox authority, and have very ambivalent memories of their training.

And that points to exactly why an Integral Buddhism—and Fourth Turning of the Wheel—is so important for today's Buddhism. Understanding both the basic structure-rungs and their Views, and the major state-realms and their Vantage Points—would in itself be an extraordinary revolution in our understanding of spirituality and its growth. States are interpreted by structures—and right there is a formula that unlocks a thousand mysteries. Incorporating that into Buddhism—or any spirituality, for that matter—would be a monumental leap forward.

## STATES AND VANTAGE POINTS

2. As the second major item, a Fourth Turning, Integral Spirituality would include *states and state-stages* (or *Vantage Points*). Most schools of Buddhism already include this (with some exceptions at magic, mythic, and pluralistic Buddhism, as we earlier suggested). But most forms of Western religion today lack *any* direct spiritual peak experiences, let alone contemplative systems spanning the entire spectrum from gross to nondual. This is odd, in many ways, because virtually all forms of Western (and Eastern) religions began as a series of mystical states and peak experiences in the founder of the religion. The very first Christian gathering—the Pentecost—was marked by massive subtle realm mysticism (flames encircling heads, at other times doves descending, and so on); and for the first several hundred years, mystical experience defined Christian awareness ("Let this consciousness be in you that was in Christ Jesus, that we all may be one"). You sought out a Christian teacher if he or she were *sanctus*—sanctified or

enlightened. But as the Church increased in power ("No one comes to salvation except by way of Mother Church"), Christianity increasingly switched from direct mystical experiences to mythic narratives, beliefs, and legalistic creeds. Mouthing the creeds replaced experiencing Spirit. By the time of the counter-Reformation, virtually all the contemplative branches of Christianity had been severely curtailed, and the Spanish Inquisition was fully in place to guard against any experiences of the Supreme Identity, or identity of subtle soul and causal God in nondual Godhead. Saints like Giordano Bruno were burned at the stake for stepping over the line, not to mention upwards of perhaps 300,000 women burned for their experiential revels, charged with "witchcraft." (The extraordinary Meister Eckhart, universally regarded as one of the greatest sages the world, East or West, has ever known, had his theses condemned by the Church, which means, I guess, that while Eckhart is now in heaven, his theses are burning in hell. That must not leave the poor man much to be thinking about. . . .)

The mythic structures of spiritual intelligence at that time—which were still adequate, as structures, for that pre-rational, pre–Western Enlightenment era—were, alas, permanently moved into place, and states were in essence banned across the board, especially since states, unlike mythic creed-beliefs, could not be controlled by the Church. The double problem with this move, in addition to losing states, was that the Mythic-Literal View of spiritual intelligence was frozen into place and made everlasting dogma, never to be questioned henceforth. As the other intelligences—in the sciences, in medicine, in law, in art, in education and politics—moved into modern rational, then postmodern pluralistic, then possibly even unifying Integral, religion remained frozen at mythic-literal—ethnocentric, racist, sexist, patriarchal, dogmatic, unquestionable. (The previous pope, Benedict XVI, announced that having women admitted as priests would be equivalent to the sin of pederasty. No offense, but which of those two has he experienced such as to be able to make such a judgment?) The Western world, in effect, ceased its spiritual growth. Spiritual intelligence—the way we GROW UP—was frozen at mythic, or that of today's typical 7-year-old; and spiritual states—the way we WAKE UP—were banned. This is, in essence, the anemic state of Western spirituality today. No wonder there has been such an avid interest in ideas such as Integral Christianity and other forms of spiritual involvement.

It should be emphasized, however, that even in those spiritual schools that put states and Vantage Points front and center, such as Buddhism, none of them historically have included structure-rungs and Views, failing to see that each state and Vantage Point will be interpreted in important ways by the View of the stage the person is at. It should be remembered that a person can be at virtually any 1st- or 2nd-tier rung— mythic or rational or pluralistic, for example—and, from that rung, meditatively develop through the entire sequence of state-stages—for example, from pluralistic gross to pluralistic subtle to pluralistic causal/witnessing to pluralistic nondual. Or from rational gross to rational subtle to rational causal/ witnessing to rational nondual. A person at, say, rational nondual, will indeed discover a pure union with his or her world—a nonduality of Emptiness and Form—but that person's world of Form only includes all phenomena up to rational. There are still "over his head" and not available in his awareness the entire pluralistic world, holistic world, integral world, and super-integral world. The individual will NOT be one with those worlds because they are completely beyond the reach of his awareness. You can't be one with that which doesn't exist in any way for you. And so over the head of this individual—who is one with the entire physical world, one with the entire biological world, and one with the mental world from sensorimotor to emotional-sexual to conceptual to concrete operational to formal operational—are the entire worlds of the pluralistic realm, the holistic realm, the vision-logic realm, and super-integral realm. If objects from any of those realms enter his awareness, he simply won't recognize them, or they will appear puzzling and nonsensical, or in other ways they just won't register. So this person having a nondual unity experience—but at mythic, rational, pluralistic, and so forth—is *not* actually one with the *entire* world (and is thus not having a *complete* unity), because there are over his head entire structure-worlds of which he is completely unaware, even though otherwise he is in a genuine nondual state of the unity of Emptiness and Form—with the caveat, "one with all of the Form that is actually in his world."

This is why it's so important for a truly comprehensive spirituality to include both structures and states. As one begins a state-development, such as meditation, one can also begin a structure-development program, such as Kegan and Lahey's work on languages and resistance to growth, or Integral Institute's meta-practice, or any variety of what Zak Stein calls "operationalizing altitude" (where "altitude" is defined as "degree of vertical [structure] growth and development"). This is important, because someone at, say, the Mythic View, who takes up Buddhist meditation and eventually moves their state center of gravity all the way to nondual Suchness, will still have the mental tools to interpret this state limited to ethnocentric modes, with a correlative belief in a "chosen people" or a "chosen path"—the belief that their path alone can deliver a true Liberation (we already saw actual schools of

Buddhism believing all of this). Even though they have taken the bodhisattva vow to liberate all beings, they can't help just having a hard time fully accepting a Muslim, or a Christian, even those with mystically nondual beliefs. The book *Zen at War* is full of examples of purely ethnocentric beliefs from highly regarded Zen Masters, showing that this is not an isolated or negligible problem.

Jeffery Martin's graduate thesis for the California Institute of Integral Studies uses Hood's Mysticism Scale (which judges consistency and type of state experiences) and Susanne Cook-Greuter's Ego Development Scale (which measures structure-stages of self-identity) to show that structure-stages do not predict any sort of correlation with state development. This is why including both state development and structure development—Vantage Points and Views—is so crucial in any effective spirituality.

SHADOW WORK

3. A third item is the *shadow* and *shadow work*. As we mentioned, few if any spiritual systems have any extensive or sophisticated understanding or models of shadow material. There is awareness of negative emotions and their effects, various defilements, even a storehouse consciousness anticipating Jung's collective unconscious by over a millennium. But specific defense mechanisms generating types of the psychodynamically repressed unconscious—this is by and large a discovery of the modern West (in many cases stimulated, ironically, by a study of Eastern systems and their complex understanding of *prana* and its vicissitudes —prana being bioenergy, élan vital, or libido—and then adding concepts like repression, denial, and the individual unconscious).

The shadow exists most basically because of the very nature of the developmental processes that the psyche goes through—in both structures and states. We've seen that in each developmental sequence, the central or proximate self first identifies with a basic structure or major state, thus seeing the world through that structure or state, hence generating a View or Vantage Point. While at this structure or state, the self needs to embrace and integrate all the major features of that dimension—all of the qualities, thoughts, feelings, needs, and drives of that structure or state. If the self fails to adequately integrate any of these elements, it will either remain fused and embedded in these elements (failure to differentiate)—thus creating an addiction to these elements (food, sex, power, etc., in the gross realm; soul luminosity and clarity, etc., in the subtle realm; archetypes in the causal realm; and so on)—or it will dis-own and dissociate from these elements (failure to integrate)—thus creating an allergy to those same elements (food, sex, power, etc.). Especially at each developmental junction—structure to structure (called a fulcrum) or state to state (called a switch-point), these types of dysfunctions are most likely to occur.

In moving from the oral to the genital stage, for example, if the self fails to differentiate adequately from oral drives, it will remain identified with or fused with those drives, thus developing an oral fixation or oral addiction, constantly substituting food for other needs and using food to generate comfort. If, on the other hand, differentiation and dis-identification from the oral stage—which is supposed to happen—goes too far into dissociation and dis-owning, then the self generates a food allergy, and thus ends up with symptoms such as bulimia or anorexia. In either case, a food subpersonality is created, which lives in the submergent unconscious and sends up constant symptoms and symbols, reading food into most of its interactions and relations. What is supposed to happen is that the oral realm (or "structure") remains, but an exclusive identity with (and View from) the oral realm is released and let go of—one still needs to eat, but one doesn't have an oral fixation. Realms remain, Views are transcended.

(As Robert Kegan summarized development—and this is true in both structures and states—"The subject of one stage becomes the object of the subject of the next." A subpersonality is a subject at one stage that refuses to become an object of the next—it's a "sub-subject," not an object. It's an "I" that won't become a "me," and thus either remains embedded in the central "I" or split off as a sub-"I," both of which are unconscious, or not a proper object of awareness. This can happen at virtually every structure, and every state, of development.)

The same thing indeed happens with states, especially at their switch-points. For example, in state development, as the self moves from the gross to the subtle, its center of gravity shifts from the gross ego to the subtle soul, or the self exclusively identified with the subtle realm and its Vantage Point (and still aware of the gross realm, just no longer exclusively identified with it—the state-realm remains, the Vantage Point is lost). Now as the self prepares to move into the causal, it must let go of itself or die to itself in order to do so. If it fears this death, the self might remain secretly identified with or attached to the soul—a soul addiction—and this soul addiction will tilt the understanding and true grasp of the causal realm. Awareness-itself will become subtly distorted. Awareness-itself will not be free of the personality but subtly attached to it and identified with it. On the other hand, if this differentiation and dis-identification goes too far into dissociation and dis-owning, a soul allergy results, where the person doesn't transcend the soul but splits parts of it off as an unconscious soul subpersonality, which it loathes, while loathing the subtle soul in general wherever it shows up—in theology, in psychology, in other people. What they hate, of course, is their own subtle soul, which they have not properly transcended but dysfunctionally dis-owned.

Now, most of these dissociated and dis-owned parts of oneself began as part of the self (a 1st-person quality, thought, feeling, or characteristic), which was then pushed away (by a defense mechanism made out of the same material as the basic rung they are at—from introjection and projection by the basic self-other boundary of the sensorimotor realm, to dynamic repression by the conceptual mind at the intentional stage, to difficulties adapting to roles or following rules at the rule/role mind, to holistic severing by vision-logic at the Integral stages)—pushed away by a rung-specific defense mechanism into an "other," a 2nd-person element in the unconscious, and often pushed even further away into a completely alien 3rd-person element (an "it" often projected onto a "him," "her," or "them"). It's a 1-2-3 process (1st-person to 2nd-person to 3rd-person).

Therefore, the 3-2-1 process developed by Integral Institute works with these shadow elements by reversing that process (not 1-2-3, but 3-2-1). Let's say, for example, that a person has a significant degree of anger (a 1st-person impulse), but for various reasons (e.g., unacceptability by parents, religion, or culture), they dissociate or push the anger out of their awareness (into a 2nd-person "other"), and then project it onto others (a 3rd-person "him," "her," or "them"). Since everybody now seems angry at this person (they know that somebody has a great deal of anger, and since it can't be them, it must be everybody else), they often develop a considerable amount of fear or depression in response. Perhaps this fear keeps showing up in nightmares as a devouring monster.

The 3-2-1 process starts by identifying the 3$^{rd}$ person that one is most reactive to, either in life or in dreams. One then faces this person (which can be either enormously positive or negative —overly admired and hero-worshipped, a projection of one's own positive qualities; or overly feared and avoided, one's own negative qualities). Facing this person, hero, or monster, one talks to it, converting it to a 2$^{nd}$ person. "Who are you? What do you want? Why are you here?" and so on, for several minutes, creating an I-Thou dialogue with this 2$^{nd}$ person. Then one takes the role of this 2$^{nd}$ person, identifies with this person or monster, speaking *as* them, until one has thoroughly re-owned and re-identified with the quality, feeling, or characteristic that this projection was holding, thus returning it to the 1$^{st}$-person element it really is. When the process is done correctly, there is usually a great sense of relief and release when finished.

Most meditators find this process easy and enjoyable. It can be done for just a few minutes each morning—with the most attractive or disturbing elements in the night's dream—and/or a few minutes before sleep—with the most admirable or irritating person during the day. And it can be done during meditation itself, when a particularly disturbing (overly attractive or particularly repulsive) item appears, disrupting mindfulness or contemplative prayer or whatever the practice is. Taking a few minutes and running through the 3-2-1 process in one's mind can rapidly clear it from awareness, allowing the practice to proceed again on track.

There is an extension of the 3-2-1 process that we call the "3-2-1-0" process, and it further involves the practice known as "transmutation of emotions." We have seen that the Tantric view of nonduality is particularly powerful, and doesn't renounce negative emotions or work to gradually transform them, but rather steps directly into the emotion with nondual Awareness, which almost instantly transmutes the emotion into its corresponding transcendental wisdom (so that anger, for example, then arises as the brilliant clarity of nondual Awareness).

But in order for this process to work correctly, the original emotion has to be an authentic emotion—meaning, even the negative emotion one is working with must really be that particular emotion, and not some displaced, repressed, or denied form of a negative shadow. But that is exactly what repression, dissociation, and dis-owning do—they fundamentally alter the emotion into a false and misleading form. Thus, in our example of dis-owned anger appearing in the dream as a monster: the monster is likely to generate emotions of fear, not anger. And it's not obvious at all that this fear is the result of a projected anger—it appears as real, genuine, authentic fear. Therefore, if one is working with transmuting emotions, one will work with fear, and work to bring nondual Awareness to bear on fear. But fear is a nonauthentic emotion; it's not real; it's not the actual emotion being originally generated (rather, anger is); and thus transmuting this inauthentic emotion will only create an inauthentic wisdom, a wisdom that is not being generated by the real and accurate energy of the original emotion, but a twisted wisdom resting on a twisted emotion. This can actually be fairly damaging, not liberating, because a false emotion is being elaborated and blown up to transcendental proportions.

But if one performs a 3-2-1 process on this fear, it will fairly quickly return to its original, authentic form of anger. And *then* if one performs the transmutation of emotions on that authentic emotion, a genuinely authentic transcendental wisdom will result (namely, brilliant luminous clarity). We call it "3-2-1-0" because, with nondual Awareness, the subject-object duality is overcome (at least temporarily), and thus "1ˢᵗ person" is transcended into "no person" or "no subject" (no subject-object duality), or "0 person." (If this practice sounds appealing, *Integral Life Practice* contains a chapter on the 3-2-1 and the 3-2-1-0 processes. Numerous books are available on the Tibetan Buddhist practice of emotional transmutation, and those can be consulted—just make sure you've first done a 3-2-1 or similar such practice to make sure you're working with the original negative emotion and not a reactive emotion to a projection.)

This is just one example of shadow work, but is often enough to handle a great deal of shadow material. If more work is indicated, a professional therapist can be consulted.

Shadow elements can be generated from virtually any View at any structure-rung and any Vantage Point at any state/realm. No matter how otherwise healthy one's structural development or how successful one's meditative state development, a shadow malformation can completely gum up the works. We know from long, hard, bitter experience in meditation, from the time of its introduction in the West some 40 years ago, that meditation won't cure shadow issues and often inflames them. We all know meditation teachers who are often superb state teachers but structurally are shadow-ridden neurotic nuts, to put it as politely as I can. Don't be a victim of your own shadow, but include at least a little shadow work along with your meditation.

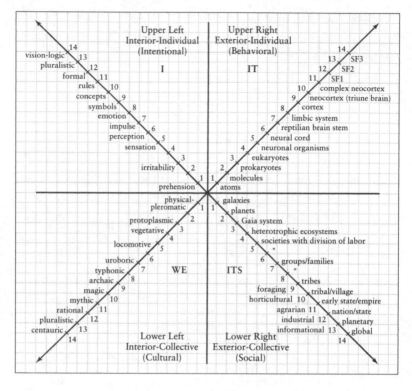

FIGURE 4.1. *Some details of the 4 quadrants.*

## QUADRANTS

4. Briefly, the 4 *quadrants* are 4 perspectives and dimensions that all phenomena possess. You can look at any thing or event from both the interior and the exterior, and in both individual and collective forms—giving 4 perspectives overall. (See fig. 4.1, the quadrants with some general details; fig. 4.2, focused on some human characteristics; fig. 4.3, showing various types of truth; and fig. 4.4, applied to medicine to give an Integral Medicine.)

As noted, these 2 dimensions (interior/exterior and individual/collective) give us 4 major combinations—the interior of

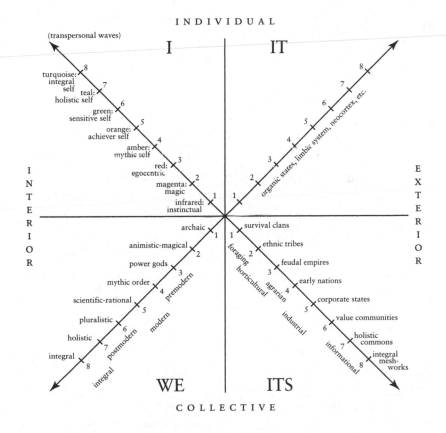

FIGURE 4.2. *AQAL.*

the individual (the "I" space, accessed by introspection and meditation; containing thoughts, images, ideas, feelings, and emotions; and whose form of truth is "truthfulness," or "When I say it is raining out, am I being truthful?"); the exterior of the individual (or "it" space, seen objectively by observation; containing atoms, molecules, cells, organ systems, lungs, kidneys, trees, animals, and the individual's behavior—all in their singular or individual form; whose type of truth is generally and simply called "truth"—as in, "Is it true that it is raining out?"

or "Is it true that water contains 1 hydrogen and 2 oxygen molecules?"); the interior of the collective (or "we" space, known by mutual understanding; containing shared values, ethics, worldviews, etc.; and whose form of truth is "cultural fit," "justness," "appropriateness," or "goodness"—as in, "What is the just thing to do with this murderer?"); and the exterior of the collective (or "its" space, involving systems and collective structures, institutions, and techno-economic modes of production, such as foraging, farming, industrial, informational, etc.; known by objective observation of collectives or systems; and whose form of truth is "functional fit"—as in, "Do these phenomena all fit well together and function as a unit?"). These 4 major dimension-perspectives are often reduced to 3, collapsing the 2 exterior realms to one objective or 3rd-person realm

|  | INTERIOR<br>Left-Hand Paths | EXTERIOR<br>Right-Hand Paths |
|---|---|---|
|  | SUBJECTIVE | OBJECTIVE |
| INDIVIDUAL | *truthfulness*<br>sincerity<br>integrity<br>trustworthiness | *truth*<br>correspondence<br>representation<br>propositional |
|  | I \| it | |
|  | we \| its | |
| COLLECTIVE | *justness*<br>cultural fit<br>mutual understanding<br>rightness | *functional fit*<br>systems theory web<br>structural-functionalism<br>social systems mesh |
|  | INTERSUBJECTIVE | INTEROBJECTIVE |

FIGURE 4.3. *Validity claims.*

(or "it"), with "you/we" being 2nd person and "I" being 1st person, giving us the "Big 3" of I, we, and it (or self, culture, and nature; or Buddha, Sangha, and Dharma).

This AQAL Framework ("all quadrants, all levels [structure-rungs], all lines [multiple intelligences], all states, all types") can be applied to any human discipline or activity, thus converting it into an inclusive or Integral version. In fact, the *Journal of Integral Theory and Practice*, the major peer-reviewed journal in the field, has published articles now in over 50 different disciplines, all re-interpreted with an AQAL Framework, thus making it an Integral version of its field—and in all 50 fields. As only one example, see figure 4.4, which is one version of an Integral AQAL Medicine (this figure shows only the quadrants, but all the other dimensions of the Framework are also included in more complete Integral Medicine versions).

|  |  |
|---|---|
| **ALTERNATIVE CARE** | **ORTHODOX MEDICINE** |
| Emotions | Surgery |
| Attitudes | Drugs |
| Imagery | Medication |
| Visualization | Behavioral modification |
| I | IT |
| WE | ITS |
| **CULTURAL VIEWS** | **SOCIAL SYSTEM** |
| Group values | Economic factors |
| Cultural judgments | Insurance |
| Meaning of an illness | Healthcare policies |
| Support groups | Social delivery system |

FIGURE 4.4. *4 Quadrants of Integral Medicine.*

Spiritually this is important because Spirit, too, can be viewed through these 3 or 4 major perspectives. And the important point is that all 3 of these perspectives are true, and all 3 need to be included in any comprehensive spirituality.

Spirit in 3rd person is Spirit looked at objectively, as in the Great Web of Life or Indra's Net. This is a very popular view in the modern and postmodern world. It is behind everything from the Universe Story to Gaiacentric views. It is often combined with systems theory (which also tends to focus on collective exteriors, or the Lower Right quadrant). It's true because it represents the objective dimensions of Spirit.

Spirit in 2nd person is Spirit conceived as a Great Thou or Great Intelligence, the universe as a living, breathing, vital, alive Reality, with which you can have a living relationship. It is also a reminder that ultimate Reality will always be, in some ways, a Great Mystery, a Great Other, that can never be known or directly identified. It is Spirit as disclosed in Martin Buber's beautiful writing on God as an I-Thou relationship, realized in gratitude and service. Metaphorically, Spirit is infinite Being, and radiant Intelligence—and a Being with Intelligence is a Person, and in that metaphorical sense, Spirit in 2nd person is that dimension of Spirit that can be approached in a personal, living relationship, an I-Thou relationship (when a spiritual teacher is considered a living embodiment of Spirit, as in guru yoga, then that teacher, as a "you," is also Spirit in 2nd person). "Conversations with God" are possible whenever the Heart opens to the Voice of the Ultimate, consents to the Presence of the Lord, and listens in all humility and openness. If the height of natural evolution is the human being—a person—why should the height of spiritual evolution be anything less? Remembering Nagarjuna's lessons, these are ultimately just metaphors for Spirit anyway—but so then is the Great Web of Life, Being-Consciousness-Bliss, Jehovah, or any other quality or positive characterization. But at least in relative truth, Spirit in 1st person or Great "I" (which we will discuss next), Spirit in 2nd person (or Great Thou), and Spirit in 3rd person (or Great "It" or Thusness) are all reminders that Spirit can be found as the Ground and Nature of all dimensions in the Kosmos—of all 4 quadrants. And to the extent we visualize, imagine, or characterize Spirit, we need to include all available perspectives and dimensions, starting with the 4 quadrants or the Big 3. God in 2nd person simply reminds us that Spirit can be found in every relationship we humans have, and that every conversation we have is the sincerest form of worship.

Now imagine that Intelligence—which gave rise to the Big Bang, and evolved into atoms and molecules and cells and living organisms, and explodes throughout the heavens as supernovas and star dust, that gave rise to Magic and Mythic and Rational and Pluralistic and Integral realms of culture, that pulses in each raindrop, shines in every moonbeam, cascades in every snowflake, and breathes in the Life of every sentient being, is now looking directly out of your eyes, touching with your fingers, listening with your ears, feeling with your senses, observing through your very Awareness—this is Spirit in 1st person, Spirit as your one and only True Self, the same and only Spirit looking out from the eyes of every sentient being alive—the same True Self (there is only one in the entire Kosmos) beating in the Heart and riding the breath of every being in existence. The very sense in you of I AMness is the same "Before Abraham was, I AM," the same I AMness prior even to the Big Bang, the I AMness that never enters the stream of time, and thus is found only in the timeless Now, and hence is Unborn and Undying, Uncreated and Unmade, Unformed and

Unfashioned, the same I AMness that is the Spirit and Self of the entire Kosmos, even until the ends of the worlds. And may I introduce you? This is your Real Self.

You can find this Real Self very simply: right now, simply be aware of what you feel is your self—your typical, ordinary, everyday self, simply be aware of it. But as you do so, notice there are actually 2 selves involved. There is the self you are aware of—you're this tall, you weigh this much, you have this job, you're in this relationship, and so on. But then there is the Self actually aware of all those objects—there is the Observing Self, the Witness, the Seer, the Looker. And the Seer cannot itself be seen. If you see anything, that's just another object, it's not a true subject, not the Real Self, not the true Seer. This Observing Self or Real Seer can never be seen as an object. As you look for the Real Seer, the true Witnessing Self—realizing it's "neti, neti"—"not this, not that"—not any object that can be seen but the Seer itself—all you will find is a sense of Freedom, of Release, of Liberation—liberation from an identity with any bunch of small finite objects. This small objective self, which can be seen and felt, isn't even a real Self, a real Subject, but just a bunch of objects that you have mistakenly identified with. It is this case of mistaken identity—identity with the skin-encapsulated ego, the separate-self sense, the self-contraction, instead of our open, infinite, free, liberated, empty Self-Awareness—that is the ultimate cause of all suffering, fear, angst, torment, turmoil, torture, terror, tears. As Philosophia said to Boethius in his distress, "You have forgotten who you are."

And who you are is pure Spirit in 1$^{st}$ person—pure Consciousness without an object; the pure Subject or Self aware of small subjects and objects; or as Madhyamika-Yogachara has it, pure unqualifiable Awareness as pure radical Emptiness, or ultimate Freedom, Liberation, Release—open, transparent, naked, radiant, luminous, infinite, timeless, eternal, without boundary, separation, limitation, lack, want, desire, or fear. And where is this True Self? It's what's reading the words on this page, or looking at me right now, and hearing my voice right now, and aware of this room right now, and looking out at this entire wondrous world which is a manifestation of its own self-liberated texture. It's the same I AMness you can feel right now; the same I AMness you felt last week, last month, last year. The same I AMness of 10 years ago, 100 years ago, a million years ago, a billion years ago, prior even to the Big Bang. Existing only in the timeless Now, 100% of it is fully present at every point of time, beginninglessly, endlessly. It's the only experience you have that never changes.

Spirit in 1st person—a Great "I"—is as important as Spirit in 2nd person—a Great "Thou"—and Spirit in 3rd person—a Great "It." Wars have been fought over which of these is the real Spirit. An Integral approach, of course, insists all 3 or 4 of them are equally real, equally important, equally to be included.

The 1-2-3 of Spirit is also, from a slightly different angle, Buddha (the ultimate "I"), Sangha (the ultimate "We"), and Dharma (the ultimate "It," or Thusness). The framework of the 4 quadrants, or the 1-2-3 of Spirit, is a simple reminder of many different other forms these fundamental perspectives come in, and a reminder to find room for all of them.

One final item about the quadrants: every item in each quadrant is evolving, and this evolution occurs simultaneously and mutually in all of them. We call this tetra-evolution and tetra-enaction and tetra-prehension. The reason is that, although the 4 quadrants are different dimensions and perspectives, they are different dimension-perspectives of the same phenomenon. They are the same thing looked at from 4 different perspectives. The fact that, for example, a certain amount of dopamine at certain synapses (or more generally, a specific brain state) in the Upper Right (or "it") quadrant appears in the Upper Left as a particular thought, emotion, feeling (or more generally, a specific consciousness state) only goes to show the complementary and interwoven and mutually enactive nature of epistemology and ontology: how one looks at a phenomenon helps co-determine the nature of the phenomenon seen, and the nature of the phenomenon seen helps co-determine what is seen. These are not two separate and siloed dimensions but two dimensions of the same Whole (which also has "we" and "its" dimensions as well). The universe is one massively interwoven Event, and the 4 quadrants (and 8 zones—each quadrant looked at from the inside-subjective or outside-objective view) are simply 4 of the more obvious examples of this fundamental interwovenness.

Integral Theory adapts a neo-Whiteheadian view of the nature of moment-to-moment existence. Namely, as each moment (or drop of experience) comes to be, it is a subject of experience (which means it has some degree of proto-consciousness, perspective, or what Whitehead called "prehension," which means to touch or feel); and, Integral Theory adds, it is a holon (a whole that is a part of other wholes), which gives it 4 drives—agency, or the drive to be an autonomous whole, and communion, or the drive to be a part, to be in relationship, are the two "horizontal" drives, operating on the same level of development, complexity, and consciousness. The two vertical drives are Eros, or the drive to move upward into higher levels of wholeness, complexity, and consciousness, and Agape, or the drive to embrace and include junior levels of wholeness, complexity, and consciousness. A molecule has agency, or the drive to be its own wholeness; and it has communion, or a drive to join with other molecules in relationship. It also has Eros, or the drive to a higher level of Wholeness, perhaps that of a cell, and Agape, or the drive to include and embrace its junior levels, such as atoms and quarks, in its own being. Each of those 4 drives has pathological versions: agency overblown produces not autonomy but alienation, separation, and isolation; communion overblown produces not just relationship but meltdown and fusion, being lost in the other. Extreme Eros is not just transcendence of the junior but fear and repression of the junior (Phobos); extreme Agape produces not just embrace of the junior but regression to the junior, ultimately to lifeless matter (Thanatos, or death-drive). Freud got that Eros and Thanatos were two major drives, but one of those is healthy, one unhealthy; he should have listed Eros and Agape for healthy drives, Phobos and Thanatos for unhealthy drives.

As each moment (with its 4 quadrants) comes to be as a subject, it prehends, feels, or includes the previous moment's subject, which consequently becomes an object. The inclusion of the previous moment or subject in the new moment's subject constitutes the determining or causal influence that the past has on the present. When the present moment includes the previous moment (now as object), that previous moment— since it is directly included in the present moment—obviously has an influence on the present moment (in all 4 quadrants). (With, of course, all 4 of them mutually interwoven and determining. If one quadrant doesn't fit with its successor, the entire holon is rendered extinct.)

But in addition to the previous moment influencing and determining the present, the present also has some degree of creativity or novelty, according to Whitehead. After embracing and including the previous moment—turning that subject into an object—the new moment or new subject adds its own degree of novelty or creativity to the mix. Now if the holon's degree of novelty is very small, the most determining item of the present will be the prehension and inclusion of the past, and thus it will appear—*appear*—as if we have nothing but strict causality and pure determination. The sciences that study the simplest holons—such as atoms and molecules—tend to take on a deterministic bent, and see the universe as a giant deterministic machine. But, as Whitehead points out, small amounts of creativity are not no amounts of creativity at all. Even atoms, for example, which have modest amounts of novelty, must have some, because they developed into molecules, a very creative move indeed (Eros in action). Sciences studying higher holons—animals, for example—rarely think of their subject matter as strictly deterministic. After all, a physicist might be able to predict where Jupiter will be 100 years from now, but no biologist can predict where my dog will be one minute from now.

Now Whitehead conceived of this prehensive unfolding as occurring between one subject-object stream. For Integral Theory, it occurs in all 4 quadrants—psychospiritual or "I," biophysical or "it," cultural or "we," and social or "its." Random mutation (in the Upper Right "it" organism) and natural selection (in the Lower Right "its" ecosocial system) is thus only one subset of a larger evolutionary operation. Creativity or Eros—the drive to higher wholes—is an inherent drive in all 4 quadrants (in fact, in all holons everywhere).

This means, among numerous other things, that your very own thoughts are entering the stream of human evolution right now, and are being carried forward moment-to-moment by tetra-prehensive unification. Your actions in all 4 quadrants are directly influencing evolution in all 4 quadrants. If a thought originates from an earlier level whose basic deep structures have earlier already been laid down as a relatively fixed Kosmic habit, that thought will influence the surface features of that level. If a thought occurs anywhere near the leading edge of evolution—in today's world, around turquoise, or vision-logic, or an Integral View—it will directly help determine the very structure of that level itself, and be passed on to all future generations as a relatively fixed level of consciousness. And that leads to a new moral or categorical imperative for each of us: act as if your behavior were to become part of a fixed structure governing all future human behavior. The form of future evolution is literally up to us: the more a particular thought or action is repeated, the stronger its morphogenetic field becomes, and the more likely it will be sedimented as a relatively fixed Kosmic groove, an actual, ontologically real groove cut into the very structure of the universe for all future generations.

There was a time, for example, in human history, when the only basic rungs and Views humans had were Archaic, Magic, and Magic-Mythic. And then a certain highly evolved soul began to think in Mythic terms. Given the generally communal structure of the Mythic View, and given that men tend toward agency and Eros, while women tend toward communion and Agape, this person was likely a woman. Be that as it may, she—operating from her Upper Left or "I" quadrant, began communicating this way of thinking to as many of her women friends as were open to it, operating through her Upper Right "it" behavior to create a "we" community capable of a Mythic View. These women communicated this View to as many of their mates as could understand, and if conditions in all 4 quadrants were favorable to this View, it was tetra-selected by evolution and passed forward in all 4 quadrants, eventually forming the basis of social institutions in the Lower Right, or systems, "its" quadrant. The more this Mythic community grew, surviving social and cultural upheavals that replaced the previous reigning View, the more, via morphic resonance, other communities were likely to pick up this Kosmic groove. At first there was considerable variation in its basic deep structures—all that was required is that it transcend and include its predecessor—but as one version was repeatedly selected more often, the more its morphogenetic field became dominant. Today, all around the world, in no matter what culture, the deep structures of this Mythic stage are the same, repeating the same essential features of that pioneering woman, name unknown, who thousands of years ago had the originality, creativity, and courage to think differently.

And so, today, we are all laying down the deep features of an Integral View. How are you contributing? Whether you are helping create it, or simply studying it, you are having an impact. Welcome to your place in history.

## TYPOLOGIES

5. Briefly, *typologies*—from the simple, such as masculine/feminine, to more complex, such as Myers-Briggs or the Enneagram—are qualities or characteristics that essentially remain the same throughout structure development and state development. If you are a type 5 on the Enneagram, for example, you tend to remain a 5 at archaic, magic, mythic, rational, pluralistic, and integral. Typologies have become increasingly important the more we have seen how dramatically different the various types really are, and that, for example, an Enneagram

type 4 and type 7 really do see different worlds, have different characteristics, drives, needs, defenses, and fears. It becomes obvious that various spiritual systems, growth technologies, therapeutic techniques, and so on essentially reflect the characteristics of the personality type of the founder or founders, and work well for those same types but not as well for other types. This is why it's important, as with structure Views, if you have an important message—or spiritual teaching—that you express what its central tenets look like at each type, as with each View. Only in this way can it be assured that the most number of individuals possible will be able to actually hear and understand the message or teaching.

Now typologies can get complicated, and considering the sheer number of them, attempting to take all of them into account is overwhelming, virtually impossible. The best one can do is select one or two typologies that are well-documented and oft-used, having demonstrated their usefulness time and again. I have two I particularly favor—the simple masculine/feminine and the sophisticated Enneagram.

Various versions of the differences between masculine and feminine are as old as humanity itself. Many—most—of these are culturally molded and culture-specific, although some very general features often show up cross-culturally, such as that men on average have a greater upper body strength and women give birth and lactate. Simple as those are, researchers such as feminist Janet Chafetz have demonstrated, using systems theory, that those two simple features alone are enough to be parlayed into significantly different sex roles in most cultures, with males tending toward the public/productive sphere and females the private/reproductive sphere, not due to any patriarchal oppression but simple biology. Most early, liberal feminists, fearing that biology is destiny, denied the importance or even existence of biological differences, believing, literally, that not all men but all humans were born equal. Legal, political, and educational equality is one thing, and a noble ideal; but overall functional equality doesn't make much sense, and flies in the face of most people's experience. Modern research into hormonal differences, for example, shows testosterone intimately connected with sex and aggression; whereas oxytocin, prevalent in females, is a powerful relationship drug, developed by evolution most likely to ensure a strong mother-infant bond, and giving women on average a much greater emotional sensitivity. I tend to joke that women recognize something like 18 degrees and types of emotion, while men recognize 2—forward and reverse.

An Integral approach is not frightened by biological differences. They pertain to only one quadrant—the exterior-individual (the Upper Right or "it" quadrant), which can be modified, molded, or even reversed by the other quadrants: social systems, cultural worldviews, and psychospiritual orientation. But taking the biological quadrant into account lets us at least acknowledge male and female differences and their different needs, strengths, weaknesses, and preferences, as recognized by modern and postmodern researchers, starting most famously, perhaps, with Carol Gilligan. As we saw, Gilligan's work suggested that men tend to reason in terms of autonomy, rights, agency, justice, and ranking; and women in terms of relationship, care, responsibility, communion, and nonranking.

This plays out in many, many different ways. Men, for example, are comfortable sitting in a fixed posture, motionless, observing their interior experiences for hours in a detached, emotionless, unflinching fashion—the same motionless, emotionless, fixed stance they have used all the way back to their time as hunters, waiting patiently for their prey to arrive. Women are often more comfortable with meditation in motion, moving and dancing, expressing their emotions as bhakti or loving devotion. Of course, both sexes can do either; it's just a matter of being aware of these native inclinations and taking them into account where appropriate. And, of course, these differences show up regularly in relationships, with men wrestling with their wandering sexual profligacy and women lamenting "the man's fear of commitment."

As important as these sexual differences are, even more impactful on the success of a relationship are the levels of development of the partners. Individuals at different levels— say, Mythic and Rational—rarely last out the year. Individuals at the same level generally do quite well, even if they differ significantly in other dimensions; but they can develop at different rates, end up a level or two apart, and wake up one morning and "just don't recognize the person next to them."

Martin Ucik, in a wonderful book entitled *Integral Relationships*, analyzes relationships from the AQAL Integral perspective. In other words, he analyzes relationships in terms of quadrants (major perspectives of "I," "we," and "it"); levels of development (or structure-rungs and their Views); lines of development (or multiple intelligences); states of consciousness; and types; and he finds that relationships can do well even if the partners differ in all of those dimensions—except one: levels of development (or structure-rungs). For individuals at different rung-levels, he has only one word of advice: "Sorry." Such, anyway, is what the evidence indicates.

But this also has significant implications for spiritual teachers and students. It is generally the case that spiritual teachers, especially meditation teachers, have developed to significantly higher *states* of consciousness than their students, at least at the beginning of the student's practice. But teachers tend to attract students on the same *structure*-level of development, and for good reason. A Rational teacher and a Pluralistic student, for example, will just have too many profound differences, and the teacher will interpret all of them as being part of the nasty, to-be-negated ego of the student, whereas the student, while finding much advice about states to be profoundly wise and useful, will find advice about structures to be wildly off the mark. As for them continuing to be in a teacher-student relationship, I'm afraid the same advice is all that can be given: "Sorry." This is another reason both structures and states need to be included in any comprehensive spirituality—helping both teachers and students determine just what advice is good, based on similar structures, and what advice is off the wall, based on dissimilar structures, as they continue to join together in advancing the student's state development.

The Enneagram is a sophisticated typology consisting of 9 basic types, whose names do a good job describing them. They are, from 1 to 9 respectively: the perfectionist, the giver, the performer, the romantic, the observer, the questioner, the epicure, the protector, the mediator. You can see from the names how different each type is, and you can probably guess they each have different good and bad manifestations, different strengths and weaknesses, different healthy and unhealthy major emotions and defenses, and different spiritual connections, among others. Some spiritual practices work well with some types; in other cases, they are positively damaging. Helen Palmer does a particularly fine job working with the Enneagram, but there are many terrific books on the subject that can be found. The point is to use the Enneagram or similar typologies to help understand exactly where the student is in his or her overall development, and tailor the teachings and practices to fit the particular personality type, so that spiritual practice isn't wasted on trying to change things that, in most cases, are just not open to change, any more than the student's height or ethnic origin is.

## THE MIRACLE OF "WE"

6. Another important item, itself starting to get a fair amount of attention, is what are generally referred to as "We" practices—that is, serious group practices of groups *as* groups, of groups taking up practices acting as a group, meant to evolve or transform or otherwise engage the entire group as a group entity. This is not just a group of individuals each doing an individual practice, but a group practicing as a group itself. There is a common saying: "The next Buddha will be the Sangha (the group of Buddhist practitioners as a whole)." In some ways, this is nothing but a mouthing of a green platitude (inasmuch as, for green, "individuality" itself is close to a sin, and only group, team, and collective activities are endorsed and actively engaged in). But in some cases, it is something much higher—it is the felt recognition that since there is already an entirely new type of "I" emerging at 2nd tier (namely, inclusive, all-embracing, and Integral—and actively appreciating all previous stages of development, a historically unprecedented first, a genuine emergent novelty), then there will also be an entirely new and different type of "We" emerging as well, made up of individuals at Integral and higher stages. What would this "We" be like? How can we engage it? What would it look like?

There has been, as noted, a fair amount of interest generated in this topic around the world, particularly in Integral circles, and several individuals who are actively exploring and experimenting with various "We" practices. Perhaps one of the earliest (at least in this historical era) and most influential was David Bohm, who maintained, in his book *On Dialogue*, that the world is in the dire state it is because of too much self-centered, fractured, fragmented thinking, and a new way of thinking—driven by dialogue, where we suspend assumptions and judgments, participate honestly and transparently, and stay connected—would open the door to more authentic, real, creative thinking capable of dealing with the world crisis. Francisco Varela (co-creator of the autopoiesis concept) and Otto Scharmer (creator of the "U-process" work, which continues this line of thinking), recommended a group process based on (1) *suspension* of past associations and knowledge; (2) *redirection* of awareness to the timeless present source and away from the object, co-enacting a group field; and (3) *letting go* (and "*letting come*"), and away from "looking for." Otto Scharmer expanded this into his "U process," which actually deals with the 3 major states of consciousness—getting a detailed overall awareness of the gross problem; shifting into subtle awareness and viewing the issue from there; then drawing on causal source, will, and creativity to allow new solutions; moving those back down into their subtle dimensions; and then finally materializing the solution in the gross realm. (Hence, gross to subtle to causal back to subtle back to gross. When I asked Scharmer if he agreed with this state interpretation of his U process, he said "100%.") Andrew Cohen recommended a type of "intersubjective yoga" (Lower Left quadrant) where the individual lets go of self-identity and instead identifies with awareness itself (and "the ground of being") and especially the evolutionary impulse itself and its urgency, and then lets this evolutionary intelligence speak through every group member. When done correctly, this is often reported as feeling like a "group enlightenment."

Olen Gunnlaugson has done considerable work on "establishing second-person forms of contemplative education," examining intersubjectivity from numerous perspectives; and, with Mary Beth G. Moze, wrote an important work, "Surrendering into Witnessing: A Foundational Practice for Building Collective Intelligence Capacity in Groups" (*Practice*, vol. 7, no. 3). The Martineaus have done significant work on "We" practices involving transparent contact with each member, opening to forms of "ours" and not "mine." Thomas Hübl has done some profound work on, for example, taking gross shadow material and reading "behind" or "beneath" it subtle and causal factors, and working with a field of a "We without a Them."

Decker Cunov and his colleagues at Boulder Integral Center have developed practices such as "circling," where members of the group are taught to focus on others and to openly, nakedly, honestly report all feelings and reactions moment to moment. This can lead to moments of extraordinary intimacy in the group as a whole. Dustin DiPerna, mentioned earlier, has been working with "We" practices that seem to involve the "We" itself evolving through several levels (conventional, personal, impersonal, interpersonal, transformational, awakened, evolutionary, and Kosmic). (While I am in general agreement with this work, it should at least be mentioned that this is a delicate and complicated issue, because the "We" itself does not possess a dominant monad but a dominant mode of resonance or discourse. What that means is that when an individual holon, such as my dog, gets up and walks across the room, 100% of its cells, molecules, and atoms get right up and move across the room as well—because of its dominant monad. But no group or collective has anywhere near that sort of control over its members, who rather "resonate" with each other depending upon their own Kosmic address or psychograph. Thus, the levels that Dustin discovered might very well be connected to a specific set of individuals with specific psychographs—all members were at green or teal or higher; all had access to higher states; all had done shadow work; and so on. It's not clear that a red group would—or even could—move through those same levels in that same order. But this is important exploratory research that I fully support.)

Terry Patten has done a good deal of important theoretical research and living experimentation with "We" practices, including many of those mentioned above, and has come up with his own particular "We" practice that he calls "Integral Trans-Rhetorical Praxis," which focuses on "uplift" and "deepening" rather than "persuading" or even "teaching." His first step is to describe, in 3$^{rd}$-person terms, the general Integral theory involved; then he switches to a type of 1$^{st}$-person confessional mode and talks about exactly how he is feeling in the moment as he tries to convey ideas that some people will find silly, threatening, unnecessary, and so on. This is an open, naked, confessional mode that shifts the stage from abstract philosophical terms to deeply personal and intimate terms. He then addresses the group in a "ragged truth telling" and invites them to adopt a similar type of dialogue. If this actually connects—sometimes it does, sometimes it doesn't—the whole process leaps into a type of hyper-space of collective intelligence, where the "We" itself seems to be learning how to process and function in this new atmosphere. At this point, every perspective (1$^{st}$-, 2$^{nd}$-, and 3$^{rd}$-person), every type of discourse (framing, advocating, illustrating, inquiring), every mode of exploration (trans-rhetorical, trans-rational, transpersonal) all can come into play, each under the aegis of this group intelligence. When it works, it generates—as do many of these practices—feelings of joy, inspiration, spiritual sacredness, creativity.

So much ragged excitement has been generated by these practices that Tom Murray, in an understandable and helpful response titled "Meta-Sangha, Infra-Sangha: Or, Who Is This 'We,' Kimo Sabe?" (in *Beams and Struts*), pointed out that much of the discussion in this area is diffuse, poorly defined, and nebulous. These various practices can, according to Murray, actually be involved in (1) feelings, (2) shared meaning, (3) state experiences, (4) an emergent collective entity, or (5) collective action. And, of course, he's right. And, in my opinion, that's exactly as it should be.

The problem confronting the "We" practices is simply the problem of evolution itself. Evolution has just barely poked its head into 2$^{nd}$ tier in individuals; of course, any number of individual "I's" at 2$^{nd}$ tier will of necessity generate a number of corresponding "We's" at the same altitude (teal or turquoise, in this case; occasionally—rarely—higher). But, as a community, we don't yet know how to reliably transform individuals into 2$^{nd}$ tier. In fact, transformation is poorly understood in psychology on the whole. We just don't know exactly what factors consistently produce transformation, and which don't. Margaret Mahler, after watching infant and child development as closely as anybody in history, finally gave up trying to spot what helped produce highly developed individuals, and concluded, "The lion's share of development rests with the infant." Parents who did what seemed to be everything wrong could still produce healthy and happy children; and parents who did what seemed to be everything right could produce mean-spirited little wretches. It was mostly up to the infant itself. This is generally not what the average liberal parent or educator wants to hear.

But, of course, it's no reason to stop trying. People are almost always drawn to "integral" approaches because they first read an account of development and its higher Integral stages, and they got a profound "Aha!" experience—"This exactly describes me!"—and in most of their cases, that's not an arrogant overestimation, but a profoundly relieving realization that they are not crazy, they are not insane, that their way of looking at the world—holistic, systemic, integrated, whole—is not off the wall, as almost everybody around them seems to think, but is in fact a genuine stage of real human development that has more depth and more height and more width than most, and they have finally found something that makes sense of this to them.

But exactly *how* they came to be at an Integral stage, no psychologist really and fully understands. Everybody has some sort of theory—for psychoanalysis, it's a consistently applied "selective frustration," giving the present level enough feedback to keep it healthy, but not enough to keep it fixated or embedded at it. For Robert Kegan, it's the right combination of "challenge and support"—challenging the present level, and supporting higher-level responses. But precisely how any of those actually applies to every action, nobody really fully understands.

At Integral Institute, we use a variety of practices collectively called "Integral Life Practice." This operates under the principle of what might be called "dimensional cross-training." Studies show, for example, that if you take a group of meditators and divide them into those doing just meditation and those doing meditation combined with weight-lifting (the overall number of practice hours the same in each group), that—according to scoring by the meditation teachers them-

selves—those doing both meditation and weight-lifting pro-
gressed more rapidly and to a greater extent in meditation
than those doing meditation alone. "Cross-training" seems to
accelerate both dimensions. So we use the AQAL Framework
and present practices in body (gross, subtle, and causal), mind,
Spirit, and shadow—and in self ("I"), culture ("We"), and nature ("It"). See *Integral Life Practice* (Shambhala Publications,
2008) if you're interested.

The point is still that, when it comes to "We" practices, all
that is certain is that with regard to the same "Aha!" experience that the individual had when he or she first discovered Integral, they absolutely know it must be possible to discover its
correlate in the "We" dimension (the Upper Left quadrant has
a correlate in the Lower Left quadrant—since all 4 quadrants
tetra-enact). They also realize that the discovery and elaboration of this "Integral We" is something of a prerequisite for
implementing Integral institutions in the Lower Right quadrant. The urgency of finding Integral "We's" thus couldn't be
greater given the general series of world crises we are facing.

But evolution moves as it does. Mike Murphy reminds
us that evolution "meanders more than it progresses," and
the same is true of the general Integral stages of evolution
themselves—and in every quadrant (I, We, It, and Its). And
again, not much more than 5% of the population is at Integral levels, and that population has not yet learned to
self-identify (i.e., most of the people at Integral stages don't
know they are at those stages). So the fact that "We" practices
can wander all over the areas pointed out by Tom Murray is
not only understandable, it's desirable. We are learning how
to address all of those areas—from feelings to shared meanings to state experiences to collective action—from Integral

perspectives, and there are as yet no guidebooks here at all. All we can be assured of is that Eros will continue its unrelenting pressure to transform in all 4 quadrants, and human beings will respond to that drive, come what may. Evolution, like so many learning processes, operates through trial and error—and so, across the Integral board—we are seeing many trials, many errors—and a slow, inexorable growth to greater Truth, Goodness, and Beauty.

One last thing about "We's" in general and "We" practices in particular. The psychograph of each individual in a particular group will be a determining factor in the depth or height that the group itself can achieve. With 5% of the population at Integral, a group with only 5% of its members at Integral will never be able to form an Integral "We"—the mutual resonance will be at considerably lower levels. Integral is sometimes described as "an elitism—but an elitism to which all are invited." And that's true. It is simply unavoidable that individuals who will find "Integral" anything attractive are largely those who are themselves at Integral levels of development in the first place, and at this time, that is relatively few (as we said, perhaps 5%). The same is true of "Integral We" practices, and these prerequisites simply must be acknowledged. Although one of the points of an Integral approach to any problem is to language that issue in as large a number of levels as possible (Magic, Mythic, Rational, Pluralistic, Integral, and Super-Integral—and this includes the "conveyor belt" of spirituality), this doesn't mean to cavalierly overlook Integral itself. The Integral level is a prerequisite for "Integral We" practices (although anybody can be invited to those practices; but realize that an "Integral" depth of the "We" will not be achieved in any group the majority of whose individuals are not themselves at Integral).

Terry Patten recognizes the importance of several prerequisites necessary to be "adequate" to the practice of "Integral We" practices. They are, he says,

> stage development in the self-related lines to "Exit Orange" [i.e., on the verge of exiting Orange for Green], "Exit Green," "Teal," or, for higher expressions of the praxis, "Turquoise" or "Indigo" levels [that's important; "higher expressions" of the "We" involve 2nd or even beginning 3rd tier]; in state-stage growth, the relaxation of strict fixation of attention in the gross "waking state" levels of mind and emotion, and a basic inner Witnessing [or causal] capacity; an ability to focus and direct attention and thus to stably rest it on others and the intersubjective field; some insight into shadow dynamics and ongoing sincere non-defensive inquiry into ongoing shadow dynamics; a basic capacity to endure discomfort and delay gratification; the integrity and courage necessary to transcend "looking good" in order to "make subject object" transparently; sufficient existential depth to be capable or remaining self-responsibly grounded while facing the world crisis and taking it seriously; and enough emotional intelligence, health, and compassion for self and others to be able to hold high levels of cognitive and emotional dissonance while remaining present with others in a fundamentally non-problematic manner as a mostly friendly benevolent presence. ("Enacting an Integral Revolution," Integral Theory Conference 2013)

All of those items—or certainly most of them—are required to establish perhaps the premier requirement of the group: the establishment of trust. This particularly demands individuals at 2nd-tier development, because those at 1st tier will not fundamentally respect anybody at any level other than their own, and thus a "rolled eyeball" group is what you get with mixed 1st-tier collectives. The capacity for "Witnessing" is also crucial, given that most "We" practices ask members to drop subject/object awareness and "surrender into Witnessing" or even Nondual states, and thus be able to remain focused and centered in the timeless Now and the presence of the freshness, aliveness, and novelty of the Present. With these types of prerequisites largely met, a fruitful "We" group exploration, experimentation, and learning process can occur.

What is particularly important for an Integral Spirituality or Fourth Turning is the realization that, just as there is an entirely new and historically unprecedented "I" space emerging (with a radically new capacity for higher inclusiveness and caring— and a deeper Enlightenment process reflecting this higher "I"), so there is a new and higher "We" space, or Sangha, that is also emerging, and it, too, is historically unprecedented in many of its characteristics (including access to fundamental forms of intersubjective intelligence never before seen or experienced by humans). There's not only a new and higher "I" or Buddha (at higher structure-rungs of existence) and a new and higher "It" or Dharma (or Truth that includes the truth disclosed not just by states but also by structures), there is also a new and higher "We" or Sangha (with an extraordinarily more inclusive nature and vibrant group intelligence).

But what is central for an Integral Spirituality is not that it focus merely on the collective "We," but that it integrate all 4 quadrants in each and every moment—the "I," the "We," and the "It"—self, culture, and nature—all brought together in the fresh aliveness and radiant Presence of the Present. The new Buddha is not going to be the Sangha, but the unification of the Buddha, Sangha, and Dharma in a single ongoing non-dual Awareness and Awakening.

## THE REAL IMPACT OF INTERIOR THINKING

7. *Thoughts are real things.* It's common to hear in Integral circles that Integral approaches aren't making much of an impact on the world. First, I disagree strongly. The gains that Integral approaches have made, even in the last 5 years, are rather startling: from an entire year's issue of the *Architectural Review* containing an article each month on an AQAL Integral reformulation of architecture itself; to the front-page review in the *New York Review of Books* using the AQAL Framework to explain the review; to the government of the United Kingdom releasing its official report on British capacity to respond to climate change, a several-hundred-page review using an AQAL Integral Framework as its basis; to Unity Church officially adopting the AQAL Integral Framework to create its main teaching of an Integral Christianity; to the creation of Ubiquity University, a worldwide university founded across the board on Integral principles; to mainstream articles and essays on Integral Medicine, Integral Nursing, Integral Economics, Integral Psychology, Integral Spirituality, Integral Criminology—an astonishing 50 disciplines in the *Journal of Integral Theory and Practice* have been completely reformulated using AQAL Integral terms (and those are just a small sampling of the advances).

But all of those miss the point rather entirely. The saying that we "are playing a game of miles and yet are seeing progress in only inches and feet" completely misses—or rather, uses a totally reductionistic notion of—what real progress actually means. All of these "lack of progress" complaints equate the real world with the mere sensorimotor world, and overlook the existence and fundamental reality of all of the interior worldspaces—from infrared to magenta to red to amber to orange to green to teal to turquoise to indigo to violet to ultraviolet—and the very real phenomena that can be found in each and every one of those very real worldspaces (worldspaces every bit as real as the sensorimotor worldspace). And then when progress isn't made in the sensorimotor world, all of the other progress being made in the other worldspaces is completely overlooked, and the whine of "no progress at all" rises up, deafeningly.

Real progress in the real world starts, in virtually all cases, by first, the creation, in a particular interior worldspace (amber, or orange, or green, etc.) of a growing set of real objects or real phenomena having to do with whatever it is that is under consideration (often a particular problem requiring a solution, or a particular invention needed, or particular approach to an issue, or some such). These objects that are created in the particular worldspace are, as I said, absolutely real and ontologically there. Where are they stored? Well, take morphogenetic fields in general. When a new protein is first synthesized, it could fold in literally thousands of different ways. But once it folds in a particular way, and once that way is repeated, then every single protein henceforth will fold in exactly the same way. Where is that "form" stored? How do the proteins know the correct form, since it's given nowhere in the protein itself? Well, we might easily say it is stored in the storehouse consciousness of the casual realm, as per the *Lankavatara Sutra*. But wherever it is, it is clearly stored somewhere in the real Kosmos, and it clearly has a *real causal impact* on the sensorimotor world—in this case, the folding of every protein of that particular type.

The same thing happened when, say, the red structure first emerged. At first, its deep structures could have gone in any number of different ways. All that was required is that they "transcend and include" their predecessors. But having done that, they could have developed in any number of quite different ways. But once they began forming in one way, red structures around the world began forming in an identical fashion. That was some perhaps 10,000 years ago; and now, today, wherever you find red around the world (and in its cognitive forms, it has been tested on everything from Amazon rain forest tribes, to Australian Aborigines, to Ukrainian workers, to Mexican nationals), in every case it has exactly the same deep structures. Where is that form being stored? Well, probably the same place the protein morphogenetic field is being stored (and we might as well say it's the causal-realm storehouse, but it is somewhere very real in the very real Kosmos).

Those red structures began as some red thoughts—some real red interior phenomena—in the Upper Left quadrant (the interior "I" space) of a handful of individuals, and through their Upper Right quadrant behavior, they communicated it to other individuals who might understand, and as those numbers grew, red "We" structures in the Lower Left quadrant (the intersubjective field) began to form—real "red We" objects or things or phenomena began to form in the Lower Left quadrant. As those continued to take hold, then around the world, as the red structure was starting to emerge in other places, its structure tended to be the same as had grown in this original group (thus, Magic cultures that emerged halfway around the world at that time emerged with the same basic deep structures, as Jean Gebser made so clear). These interior objects were real forms having a real causal impact on other beings around the world. And as these interior red objects continued to build, and individuals continued to think in red terms, those objects eventually spilled out of individuals' interiors and began to create material, sensorimotor, social institutions in the Lower Right. Actual empires began to form, and each in turn, particularly as it gave way to amber, conquered most of the known world in its time.

All of that came from interior thoughts as utterly real objects or ontologically real phenomena—stored in their primary forms somewhere in the real Kosmos, and reaching down and having an absolutely real causal impact on the sensorimotor world (just as the form of the folding protein reaches down and creates the form of every single one of those proteins wherever it occurs). And so creativity would go. When representative democracy first began in the modern West, it was just a thought in the minds of a few Renaissance thinkers— the notion of "individual freedom" was novel indeed, at least in that era, with amber mythic-membership conformity and monarchical rule the general order of the day. But a handful of individuals began creating internal orange objects— worldcentric objects, rational objects, trans-mythic objects. Did they run out and create a democratic revolution on the spot? Of course not. The internal objects weren't nearly clear enough yet in all their forms. And, in fact, it would take a few hundred years of continuing to build these orange interior objects—real phenomena in the real orange worldspace—that had the names of "individual freedom," "democratic representation," "nonmonarchical government," and so on.

Those interior thought objects continued to grow, up to the Paris salons and "café society" where these orange objects began to inhabit a larger and larger number of orange "We" spaces, and became real objects, real phenomena, in the orange "We" worldspace. And finally, after several hundred years of interior object building, those objects spilled out into the sensorimotor world with the American and then French Revolution, creating institutions in the Right Hand quadrants that were materializations of the orange interior objects of the Left Hand quadrants, which had been building and building for hundreds of years—and stored in the real Kosmos, eventually to have absolutely real effects.

Individuals clamoring for "Integral progress" are like those who, during the Renaissance, as orange "individual freedom" objects began to first form, would run out in the streets and try to start a democratic revolution right there on the spot, simply because a few of them thought that was a grand idea. The problem is that the idea hadn't yet had the time, nor the number of individuals, to continue to build and build internal objects representing individual freedom and representative government. It would take hundreds of years for those ideas, those internal objects, to become fleshed out enough, and elaborate enough, and complex enough to be able to create forms that, wherever they were stored in the Kosmos, would one day be able to reach right down and hammer the sensorimotor world into submission.

And so it is with Integral. Every time you think an Integral thought; every time you read or write an Integral sentence; every time an Integral feeling runs through your body—every single time, you are building internal Integral objects that are being literally stored in the real Kosmos—and one day will have such force that they, too, will reach down from their storage area and pound the sensorimotor world into submission. And that will be directly *because* of those thoughts that *you* had; those ideas that ran across *your* mind; those feelings that made *your* heart beat a little faster. Progress? Progress!!! You are engaged in one of the most

monumentally progressive movements that has ever been
seen in history. Your very activity in your consciousness is
building internal objects and ontologically real phenomena
of an Integral nature that are literally being stored in the real
Kosmos and that will one day reach down and bring men
and women to their knees with joy and gratitude and grace,
and will rewrite history as we know it, and will shape the
world with a greater Truth and Goodness and Beauty than
has ever been conceived or seen or known.

YOU, my friend, are—by every Integral thought that you
have, or conceive, or read, or write, or share, or hear, or pass
on, or dream, or envision—by the very fact of your interiorly
entertaining that Integral object of awareness—YOU are driv-
ing a progress that will one day bring the world to a shudder-
ing surrender of gratitude and grace and all-caring embrace.

Nobody knows how many interior Integral objects are
required in the "I" and the "We" before they begin to spill
out into the sensorimotor world and hammer it into a new
form the likes of which have never been seen. But consider the
sheer magnitude of that transformation in literally all walks
of life—and you think we aren't *progressing* enough??? Have
you *any* idea of what is happening here? Have you the slight-
est notion of the far-reaching transformations that your own
internal Integral thoughts are in the process of building? Run
out and start a revolution now? Are you insane? Have you really thought through the massive changes in government, education, medicine, politics, law, business, technology, energy,
food, transportation, law enforcement, the justice system—
to name a pitiful few—that will be required for this Integral
revolution?

And yet . . . it is a certainty. We know this because every
developmental model we have has, beyond the pluralistic/

relativistic stage of development, a holistic/integral stage of development. This revolution is built into the very fabric of human growth, development, and evolution. Its deep features, at least in its early forms, have been laid down (enough to show up on test after test after test). You have already thought enough interior Integral thoughts to build enough Integral objects to reach down from their Kosmic storage bin and causally influence developmental schemes and tests. This is a level that is already laid down in the Kosmos as a stage headed our way. It is a tsunami that is, today, still thousands of miles offshore—but it's headed in this direction, and nothing can stop it. That's the thing about stages of human development—real stages are given, they cannot be skipped, bypassed, or altered by social conditioning. Their deep structures are Kosmic grooves—actual ontological grooves cut into the universe by repeated human actions—and are as real—and unalterable—as Jupiter's orbit, an electron's structure, or the mechanism of DNA action.

What human actions? Why, yours, of course. Integral thinking is, on any sort of even modestly wide scale, not much older than 15 or 20 years—just about as long as many of you have been interested in it, in other words. *In other words*, it has been in the past—and certainly is right now—your thoughts and ideas and visions and works that have been building these Integral deep structures, to the point that their basic (teal) forms are being set as Kosmic grooves—and therefore are coming our way, like it or not, want it or not. Ever since you had your first Integral encounter, you have been building the interior objects that have coalesced into a set of deep structures now stored as Kosmic grooves and cut into the universe irrevocably, ready to descend onto the sensorimotor world with a thunderous crescendo that will shake people to their deepest cores, and in every known area of human activity (just as have, for example, amber and orange and green before it). Look at the world around you, and behold the landscape, behold the site, where the revolution is about to occur, and shudder with the realization of what you have accomplished in this little amount of time. The Integral changes that have already occurred have happened in lightning speed, in evolution's terms. Expect this to speed up on occasions, slow down on others—as evolution continues to meander more than progress. But don't overlook the stunning progress that has already occurred, and is continuing to occur as individuals—and "We's"—continue to grow interior Integral objects that are set to refashion the world at large.

And what can you do to help bring this historical revolution? Right now, this moment? Every time you think an Integral thought; every time you conceive an Integral idea; every time your pulse quickens with the thought of a more beautiful, more truthful, more ethical world tomorrow; every time you read and study, or create and write, of Integral notions; every time you even ask, "What can I do to bring this about, to speed this up?"; every time you dream the dream of a more inclusive tomorrow, the dream of a more harmonious future, the dream of a more balanced and cherished Earth, the dream of a Spirituality that touches the God in each and every being alive, and gives that God an embodied home in your own being; every time you reach out for a future that is even just a little more Whole than the one today; every time you imagine any human activity—from education to parenting to medicine to government to law—redrawn in a more inclusive and Integral fashion; every time you look into the eyes of a young child, perhaps even your own, and wish for them a future of greater love and compassion and care and concern, and see them smile in the radiant halo of that embracing tomorrow; every time you think a moment a little more Whole than the previous one, or see partialities brought together in the patterns that connect, or reach out to a future where all God's children are judged in Kosmic terms, not parochial or prejudiced ones; every time you make a choice that is in favor of the betterment of humankind and all living beings in their entirety; every time you see broken pieces and fractured shards and torn and tortured human beings brought together in a more unified and inclusive and caring embrace; and every time you yearn for a tomorrow even slightly more unified and inclusive and embracing than today—every time, every single time, you do anything like any of those, you are yourself directly, immediately, and irrevocably building interior Integral objects that are instantly being stored in the real Kosmos, adding a few inches to the size of that tsunami racing in our direction now. And, doing so, as we noted once before, welcome to your place in history. It is richly deserved.

---

Well, those are 7 of the most central items I would suggest are present in any Integral Spirituality, and this would include any Fourth Turning of the Wheel of Dharma. All of them are important. States, of course, are central, our very means of WAKING UP. But perhaps as important, in some ways more important, given their almost complete lack of inclusion in any spiritual system today, is basic structure-rungs and their Views. There are examples of all of the world's great religious traditions at virtually all of the levels of Views available, 1st to 2nd tier (as we have already seen with Buddhism). But the fact that they are different-level Views is not understood—they are all taken to be working with the same "God" or the same

"Spirit" or the same general religious landscape in general, and that is simply not the case—most of them are representing different-level Views of spirituality. Including structures and their Views in one's spirituality will allow this fact to be taken into account, and become part of the overall "conveyor belt" of the particular spirituality, where the fundamental root insights of that spirituality are expressed in the language, perspectives, and Views of each major structure-rung of development, thus becoming part of the individual's "vertical" transformation from stage to stage to stage, starting in early childhood and ending in the late maturity of the sagely aged individual.

Plus, as more and more people enter the Integral stages themselves, there will be a greater and greater demand for all things Integral—Integral business, Integral education, Integral medicine, Integral politics, Integral spirituality. The demands to move from the limitations of $1^{st}$-tier stages (Mythic to Rational to Pluralistic) to the fullness of a $2^{nd}$-tier Integral View will become greater and greater.

The advantages of this move are legend, as we have been pointing out. I'll outline only a few, just as a summary. In including all 4 quadrants, the war between science and spirituality is ended. The Right Hand quadrants, whose validity claims include truth and functional fit, cover all the major sciences—physics to biology to chemistry to ecology to sociology—and the Left Hand quadrants—whose validity claims include truthfulness and justness—cover all major aspects of spirituality, from structures to states. The Right Hand quadrants include a spectrum of mass-energy (gross energy to subtle energy to causal energy) and the Left Hand quadrants include a spectrum of consciousness and culture (including Views, Vantage Points, art, morality, typologies, shadow elements, therapies, and so on). A spectrum of development, in all quadrants, allows every major discipline to be coordinated with human growth and evolution. A view that includes all quadrants, all levels, all lines, all states, and all types makes room for everything in the Kosmos, and generously includes it. Ultimate Enlightenment—and the ways we Wake Up; relative lines—and the ways we Grow Up; shadow therapies—and the ways we Clean Up; and Unique Self—and the ways we Show Up: there is a warm outreach and glad inclusion of them all.

Such would be true of a Fourth Turning in Buddhism as well. Buddhism, which throughout its history has shown strong interests in evolutionary and integrated and systemic ways of thinking, along with a panoply of profound practices for awakening, is ready for yet another profound unfolding, retaining all the essentials of its previous Turnings and adding the new elements that have unfolded as Spirit-in-action has continued its unrelenting evolution.

*Part Three*

# THE FUTURE

# 5

## THE FUTURE OF BUDDHISM

Wʜᴀᴛ ɪs ᴛʜᴇ ғᴜᴛᴜʀᴇ of spirituality, particularly our main topic, Buddhism? If we focus on structures of consciousness for a moment, and compare them with states, we note a point we made at the start: there are at least two very different forms of spirituality and spiritual engagement. The first, focused on structures—and that means spiritual intelligence—is essentially a belief system, a narrative or series of stories, a philosophy of life. What has become absolutely obvious in the past few decades is that there are stages to these beliefs—moving, in our simplified form, from archaic to magic to magic-mythic to mythic to rational to pluralistic to integral and super-integral. The differences between the earlier and junior stages—up to, say, ethnocentric mythic-literal—and the later and senior stages—rational worldcentric and higher—are as stark as night and day. It's hard to believe they are both referred to by the same terms, such as "religion" and "spirituality." (The same is true of structures themselves in general, and of states, which we will get to in a moment.) You can see this evolution of Views in the Bible itself, where in the early sections of the Old Testament, God is mean-spirited, vengeful, hostile, murderous, jealous, racist, sexist, and generally malicious. There are over 600 passages alone where God directly recommends violence or murder, and He plays with people's lives—like Job's or those of Abraham and his son—in the most frivolous and cavalier of ways. By the time we get to Jesus— who is moving from egocentric and ethnocentric into world-centric—we find Divinity recommending love of one's enemies and turning one's cheek, and claiming the meek shall inherit the earth. This is quite an evolution, and there in print, plain as day, for all to see.

We notice much the same type of evolution in all the religions that began at magic, magic-mythic, or mythic/ego-centric or ethnocentric. Those characteristics of God I just mentioned are not genuine characteristics of true Divinity, but Divinity as it appeared to humans two and three thousand years ago, reflecting more than anything the characteristics of the archaic, magic, and mythic structures. Most of the religions that began at those early stages became fixated at the mythic stage, both East and West. This was appropriate up to the Renaissance, but beyond that, represented a culture-wide case of arrested development in spiritual intelligence. This has become increasingly problematic on a worldwide scale, because the mythic and lower stages are ethnocentric at best, and that means the world—some 70% of which is at mythic ethnocentric stages or lower, and most of that 70% is religious in origin and meaning, adopting a mythic or lower spiritual view—remains culturally divided into heavily fortified camps (psychologically and/or physically), bent on mutual intolerance at best and jihad (holy war) at worst, the deep-seated belief that my religion alone is truly real and truly capable of a genuine salvation. Even religions that have officially adopted a rational worldcentric View, such as the Catholic Church after Vatican II (during which the Church officially announced that other world religions might indeed offer a similar salvation as that of Christianity, a monumental move from amber ethnocentric to orange worldcentric), often have a majority of members that remain fixated at the mythic-literal View, simply due to the Church's overall attitude and tone remaining Mythic, and a lack of enthusiasm for worldcentrically sharing salvation equally with the world's other great religions. The two popes preceding Pope Francis certainly seemed to do everything in their power to reverse Vatican II.

As the world's sciences, arts, and humanities race through Rational and Pluralistic, and now stand on the verge of a revolutionary Integral, most religions have proudly dug in their heels at Mythic and ethnocentric, guaranteeing that it is the case that religion will remain the world's single greatest force—beyond even racism—for conflict, disharmony, lack of love (despite their public relations to the contrary), war, and terrorism. Most terrorism, in fact, for the last 30 years, has been religiously driven, not politically. Going back 30 or 40 years ago, almost any time terrorism was committed, it was by groups such as the Red Army Faction, the Baader-Meinhof Gang, or the Palestine Liberation Army. Starting about that time, the organizations committing terrorism were more often religious fundamentalists—including groups like Hamas and al-Qaeda as well as members of virtually every major religion: Southern Baptists bombing abortion clinics; Buddhists putting sarin gas in the Tokyo subway system; Sikhs and Hindus fighting over Pakistani borders; Buddhists and Tamil Hindus fighting over the real spiritual truth. Science takes up a stance on this side of the rational worldcentric divide, and religion a stance on the lower side, as mythic ethnocentric, and that utterly ridiculous debate (rational science versus mythic religion) is at the very core of our culture wars, when the religious faction doesn't spill over into actual terrorism.

The problem runs deeper. Even the higher stages of spiritual intelligence, as utterly and crucially important as they are, do not in themselves deliver a genuine spiritual liberation, awakening, and Enlightenment. For this, state development is required. This has always been one of the strengths of most schools of Buddhism, which we'll return to shortly. The problem is the large number of religions that rely on structures alone, on spiritual intelligence only (let alone those relying on merely its Mythic stage). Spiritual intelligence offers only relative truth. As such, it combines with other multiple intelligences— moral, interpersonal, emotional, cognitive worldviews, intra-personal, among others—to guide the separate self on its journey through life. But it does nothing to transcend the separate self into the Real Self, the Self as ultimate Spirit, pure Thusness or Suchness. It does nothing directly, in other words, to open one to ultimate Truth, the Ground and Goal and Suchness of evolution itself—cosmic to personal. The unique role that spirituality plays—the awakening, via state-stage development, of one's Supreme Identity with ultimate Spirit itself—is completely lost. The ultimate core of a human being—pure unqualifiable I AMness as such—is not even recognized, but mistaken as a small self, an object or collection of objects, there to take its pitiful place with all the other small, finite objects in the universe, that all live, suffer, are tormented, tortured, and die. The Unborn, Unmade, Uncreate, Undying, Loving, and Joyously blissful core of Being goes unrecognized and unrealized, and with it, ultimate Reality. Life passes by as a dream, a bubble, a mirage, an image shimmering in a desert of suffering, and no one is the wiser. Spirituality's one, true, unique, and radical purpose withers.

Buddhism's central strengths have always been twofold: first, with regard to structures, it was born a Rational world-centric religion (take nothing on mythic authority, but tested in personal experience and reason); and second, it puts states front and center. Of course, not all schools of Buddhism—and certainly not all students—have risen to these auspicious beginnings (let alone moved beyond them). Many schools and students (as we have seen), are firmly at Magic or Mythic. Now it's entirely appropriate, in an overall conveyor belt, that younger students pass through Magic and Mythic stages of Dharma teaching. As long as the higher stages are clearly announced and emphasized—and, hopefully, as long as Buddhism continues its own conveyor belt and moves into a 2nd-tier, Integral, evolutionary Fourth Great Turning, ensuring that the teachings of Buddhism keep pace with the evolution of Spirit and Dharma itself—then having Magic and Mythic stages of Dharma teaching is entirely appropriate, just as long as they alone are not believed to exhaust or fully capture the teaching.

This goes for every stage of View available. As it is, and as we earlier discussed, the majority of Buddhist teaching in the West is centered on the Pluralistic View of spiritual intelligence (along with causal and nondual states, its saving grace). But the Pluralistic View, like all 1st-tier Views, believes that its truth and values are the only real truth and values in existence. Further, since structure Views (unlike state Vantage Points) cannot be seen by introspecting, the contemplative and meditative traditions are largely unaware of the existence of these structures and their evolving Views (again, unlike states, which they have often mapped quite fully). Therefore,

Buddhism (along with other religions) tends to identify the Dharma with its present View, unknowingly—which, in most cases in the West, as we were saying, means Dharma is equated with the Pluralistic View (while conventional Western religion is identified even lower, with its Mythic View). And this, truly, is a disaster for Buddhism (not to mention typical conventional religion), because Dharma then becomes interpreted exclusively through the Pluralistic lens. Dharma thus inherits not only the positive truths of the Pluralistic View (its sensitivity, care, interest in civil rights, environmentalism, feminism, and sustainability), but also its negatives and limitations: it is a 1st-tier View, and thus fragmented; it is anti-all hierarchies and not just anti-dominator hierarchies, and hence is reluctant to acknowledge any growth or actualization holarchies, and hence tends to deny any developmental maps, in structures or states (despite the abundance in all schools of Buddhism of state-stage maps); because of its strong allegiance to the Pluralistic View, it thinks pluralistic truths are the only possible truths there are, and thus often equates pluralistic views not only with relative truths, but with ultimate Truth itself (and thus, e.g., will equate Emptiness with nonhierarchies, whereas Emptiness is neither hierarchical, *nor* not hierarchical, nor both, nor neither); because of its attachment to Pluralistic views, it fails to use universal integrating vision-logic (of 2nd tier), whereas most of the geniuses of Buddhism made abundant use of vision-logic (from the aforementioned *Lankavatara Sutra* to Longchenpa to Tsongkhapa to Fa-tsang, to mention only a few). This lack of integrative knowledge further acts to keep Dharma locked in its 1st-tier prison (along with the pluralistic correlatives of 1st-tier arrogance, antihierarchicalism, anti-intellectualism, antiauthoritarianism, anticonceptualism, and other merely stage-specific partial Views that deeply cripple Buddhadharma and its chance of evolving into the post-postmodern world). Before his untimely death, Traleg Rinpoche and I were working on a book, *Integral Buddhism*, which addressed these serious limitations of Buddhism as generally practiced in the West (and East), hoping to thereby help students and teachers alike move out of this Pluralistically identified View and into more $2^{nd}$-tier, genuinely holistic and Integral Views, thus keeping pace with the evolution of Buddhanature and Spirit itself.

The hope, then, as far as it goes with structures and states, is that Buddhism begins to complement its strong understanding of state-realms with structure-rungs and their Views. After all, as we have seen, everything from individual students and teachers to entire schools of Buddhism already exist at Magic, Mythic, Rational, Pluralistic, and Integral stages of structural View. This is *already* occurring, and thus the hope is that, instead of doing this blindly and unconsciously, as now happens, it is done explicitly and consciously, thus creating a great conveyor belt of structural transformation, so that Buddhism would not only help individuals move through the various major states of consciousness (gross to subtle to causal to witnessing to nondual), but also act as a great pacer of transformation, ideally picking individuals up at the earlier structure-rungs of existence (magic and mythic), and helping them move into the higher, wider, deeper rungs as well (rational, pluralistic, and integral). Buddhism (and other equally comprehensive spiritual systems) would thus play an important, even central, role not only in helping humans Wake Up, but also in helping them Grow Up.

And most importantly, by including an understanding of structures and structure-stages, Buddhism would be open to moving into $2^{nd}$ tier and thus be an intrinsic part of the revolutionary integral transformation starting to sweep the planet. If it fails to do so, and remains at 1st tier, it risks running the disaster, in relationship to science, that the Christian Church did (and still does). Namely, as the worldcentric Rational structure emerged, the Catholic Church remained behind at Mythic, thus becoming the laughingstock of reasonable men and women everywhere (Parted the Red Sea? Born of a virgin? Rained down blood? You've got to be kidding me!). Science (and art and ethics, etc.) moved forward, religion remained behind, and began mostly appealing to lesser-developed and lesser-evolved souls ever since. Science (art, ethics, etc.) is already moving into 2nd tier; Buddhism should continue its own growth and evolution with it. Buddhism, unlike most other religions, has never had any problems with science—they were both born at the Rational level (both depended on personal experience, evidence, experiment, and reason, not mythic authority and dogma). It would be a pity to see science and Buddhism go their separate ways, science moving into revolutionary 2nd tier and Buddhism remaining behind at an outmoded 1st-tier stance.

This is especially so as science continues its monumental research into brain function and neurophysiology. Although science still tends to deny interiors—and thus deny the "I"-space that is Buddhism's specialty (the Upper Left is the home of structures, states, and shadow; and science continues to focus on the Upper Right, from string physics to molecular biology to brain states). But brain states, via quadrant tetra-enaction, directly affect consciousness states (not to mention consciousness structures and shadow). Already brain technologies such as binaural beats and trans-cranial stimulation can generate alpha, theta, and delta states, which are Upper Right correlates of Upper Left gross, subtle, and causal consciousness states, respectively. We can already, in a matter of minutes, put a person into theta/subtle states and delta/causal states, which sometimes takes meditators many months to accomplish.

The inclusion of all 4 quadrants in any spiritual system includes a theoretical way to include these facts with no contradictions or difficulties. And these types of discoveries are going to continue. Long-term Tibetan monks, practicing forms of compassion meditation, have already been determined to produce significantly more gamma brain waves than others—yet another important meditative state that can now be produced in a matter of minutes instead of months or years.

I have no doubt that neurotransmitter profiles of different meditative states (*savikalpa samadhi, nirvikalpa samadhi, jnana samadhi, sahaja samadhi,* and so on) will soon be determined as well, giving yet another brain state access to corresponding consciousness states. This is yet another reason that all religions need to be on speaking terms with science, and have a sophisticated meta-theory, such as the quadrants, that directly and seamlessly connects scientific truths with spiritual truths. And this does not include silly claims like quantum mechanics proves mysticism. These are two different realms entirely, with quantum mechanics dealing with subatomic particles in the lower levels of 3rd-person Upper Right quadrant, and mysticism referring to higher reaches of 1st-person states in the Upper Left. If they were dealing with the same realities, then to master quantum mechanics would make one a great mystic, whereas the vast majority of professional physicists are no such thing. They fully understand quantum mechanics but are clueless when it comes to real mystical states. Further, mysticism is one of the simplest experiences humans can have—for example, the experience that "All is One"—the utter simplicity of that Oneness is breathtaking when you experience it. Quantum mechanics and its Schrödinger wave equation, on the other hand, is one of the most complex and convoluted systems of thought ever devised by humans (as one pioneering physicist put it, "Anyone who claims to have understood quantum mechanics cannot possibly have understood it"). No, an understanding of science and spirituality means understanding how they are related, but also why they are different disciplines, with different methodologies, different techniques, different modes of knowing, and different disclosures—*and*, how all of those are noncontradictorily interrelated. (This can include an understanding of the mystical oneness of science and spirituality, a mystical territory itself given only by spirituality, while science gives, at best, maps of that territory, and to claim they are the same is to confuse map and territory.) Integral Theory and the AQAL Framework claims to perform this integration smoothly. But whatever theory or meta-theory is used, it's a task that needs to be included in any spirituality of tomorrow—and starting now.

Any Buddhism of a Fourth Turning (and any complete spirituality in general) will also need to include at least a brief overview of the shadow and techniques for addressing it (or, alternatively, a formal relationship with an established psychotherapeutic professional individual or group to which students who have shadow issues can be referred). Roger Walsh, MD, PhD, is both a psychiatrist and an Integral Buddhist teacher. He estimates that perhaps 80% of the questions that come to him in private student-teacher consultations during meditation retreats are best handled by therapeutic techniques, not meditative techniques. I think that's generally valid, and if so, that means that 80% of the advice being given to students by meditation teachers is less-than-optimal (not to mention the previously discussed disaster that the majority of advice is also coming from the Pluralistic View, no matter what View the student presently holds). That is a catastrophe in itself, and can only be remedied as Buddhism becomes Integral Buddhism and includes structure-rungs and their developing Views in its overall teaching—which is, of course, one of the main recommendations for any Fourth Turning Dharma.

But no matter how structurally evolved or state-evolved a person may be, a nasty shadow issue can screw the whole psyche up, not to mention one's practice and life in general. And, as we have noted, few if any spiritual systems—especially of the major religions—have any sophisticated understanding of the dynamically repressed shadow.

Allow me a few brief words on personality types and typologies. If one is any sort of coaching counselor in the broadest sense (using "coaching" to apply to everything from meditation teacher to contemplative prayer teacher to psychotherapist or yoga instructor), the brief study of any sophisticated typology—from Myers-Briggs to the Enneagram—will show immediately how different the coaching program needs to be for different personality types. Somebody who is a type 5 on the Enneagram—"the Observer"—might all too easily get caught up in extreme or dysfunctional Witnessing in a meditation of that type, as the practice of Witnessing conjoins with the personality type of witnessing or observing to give a thoroughly overblown state of dysfunctionally detached and depersonalized awareness, generating a great deal of difficulty making authentic contact and feeling the manifest world and one's own emotional states—at worst leading to a depersonalized schizoid position. This person would do better with, say, contemplative prayer, loving-kindness meditation, or tonglen, all of which increase authentic emotional contact, not diminish it. But this is just another example of what an Integral approach in general does—namely, gets rid of a "one-size-fits-all" approach, which flattens the genuine differences between people and smooshes them all into the same category with the same unimaginative practice. The extraordinary differences between people have been one of the most significant discoveries of the Integral approach.

Again, we don't need to go overboard here. The complexities are immense, and it's easy to get lost in them. That's the point of the AQAL Framework—to use the fewest number of dimensions to explain the most amount of reality. The same should be true of typologies: pick one that is detailed enough (say, 6 to 9 types) to cover a great deal of ground, and then essentially stick with that; don't go trying to mix and include four or five typologies into a staggering number of overly complex types (although there is nothing in the "integral rule book" that flat-out prevents you from doing so if you want). But one good typology—say, the Enneagram or Myers-Briggs—can do wonders in helping to fine-adjust a practice for different personality types.

In the ultimate Nondual traditions, nonduality is metaphorically described as the nonduality of subject and object, or infinite and finite, or eternity and time, or samsara and nirvana, or ultimate and relative, or Spirit and matter, One and Many, or—perhaps most often—the nonduality of Emptiness and Form. As the *Heart Sutra* puts it, "That which is Emptiness is not other than Form; that which is Form is not other than Emptiness."

Emptiness is a state discovery. That is, by moving through and transcending all lower or junior states, until all phenomena—gross, subtle, and causal—are transcended, all that is left in the highest state-condition is—metaphorically—pure Emptiness, Openness, Transparency, Nothingness, Vast Spaciousness: the discovery of which confers ultimate Freedom, Liberation, Release, moksha, wu, metanoia, Liberty—Unbound, Uncreate, Unborn, Unmade, Undying. The discovery of this Emptiness is infinite Freedom from all finite objects and any identity with, or grasping of, those objects—whether gross objects, subtle objects, or causal objects: all are transcended and let go.

But this Emptiness is not-two with the world of Form—the ultimate Nondual estate transcends and includes the entire world of Form. And where Emptiness is a matter of states and Freedom, Form is a matter of structures and Fullness. And while Emptiness has not changed since the Big Bang or before, Form and Fullness have changed, as the universe continued to evolve into more and more complex Forms, hence becoming Fuller and Fuller. As we noted earlier, we can see the universe get Fuller and Fuller as it evolves from subatomic particles to atoms to molecules to cells to organisms, and from there to photosynthetic organisms, to organisms with neural nets, to ones with reptilian brain stems, to limbic systems, to the triune brain, whose neural synapses outnumber all the stars in the universe. The interiors of these holons have been evolving into more and more complex, Fuller and Fuller forms, as well, from prehension, to protoplasmic irritability, to sensation, perception, impulse, image, emotion, to—with humans—concepts, schema, rules, formal meta-rules, vision-logic, para-mind, meta-mind, and higher (pushing into over-mind and supermind).

These basic holons supported various worldviews, as we have seen, starting, in humans, at image and impulse with Archaic, and moving to Magic, Mythic, Rational, Pluralistic, Integral, and Super-Integral.

But this leads to an inescapable conclusion: when compared to the Enlightened sages of, say, 3,000 years ago, whose dual center of gravity was generally Mythic, Nondual—giving them the benefit of the doubt about being Nondual instead of the more common causal at that time—a fully Enlightened sage of today is not more Free (Emptiness is still the same Emptiness, and hence the same Freedom), but he or she is Fuller (since there have evolved, from the time Mythic was the highest structure, at least 3 new and higher structures—Rational, Pluralistic, and Integral—which today's fully evolved sage would include). Enlightenment, in other words, is being one with both the highest state and the highest structure to emerge at a given time in history. Assuming both sages achieved the Nondual state (although it is more likely the early sage achieved causal at best), the earlier sage achieved at best Mythic, and there are, "over his head," so to speak, at least 3 higher very real structures of the Kosmos (Rational, Pluralistic, and Integral) that the earlier sages are *not* one with, because those haven't emerged or evolved yet in any significant fashion. Today's sage, on the other hand, realizing the same nondual Emptiness, is no Freer than the early sage, but is definitely Fuller, having included in his Supreme Identity at least 3 higher ontologically real levels of the Kosmos. The Emptiness of both confers the same Freedom, but the greater and more complex Form of the latter gives the modern sage a significantly greater Fullness, or more Being.

And this is something a Fourth Turning of the Wheel would want to take advantage of. Emptiness and Form are still nondual or not-two, but the world of Form has evolved, following that inexorable "creative advance into novelty," and therefore the very identity of our modern sage is Fuller—actually contains in his or her being up to 3 or 4 greater levels of Reality, and a correspondingly greater, Fuller degree of Being. Of course, our modern sage might only be at Magic structurally, and hence would have less Fullness then our ancient Mythic sage. But by defining "Enlightenment" as being one with all states and all structures that have emerged and evolved at a given point in history, the evolved sage of today would be no Freer, but significantly Fuller, then yesterday's sage.

And that is perhaps the last item that we would want to include in any Buddhism undergoing a Fourth Turning. Evolution carries on. Spirit-in-action carries on. The unfolding of higher and higher, more complex and more complex, structures of Reality carries on. And since Enlightenment involves a oneness with the entire universe, Enlightenment itself becomes richer and richer, what Whitehead called (in contrast to the "Primordial Nature of God," or unchanging Emptiness) "the Consequent Nature of God," which becomes Fuller and Fuller, and hence so does a oneness (or not-twoness) with that God (while the Freedom with the Primordial Nature of God remains unchanging). By including structure-rungs and their Views, the Fullness of Buddhanature (and not just its Freedom) becomes able to be tracked, thus increasing the Depth of our Enlightenment and the Degree of our Awakening, one of the primary goals of Buddhism from its very inception.

A Fourth Turning of Buddhism is consistent with its history and its own self-understanding, and has much to recommend it. I join those students and teachers who argue that now, indeed, the time is ripe for such a Turning. The world is on the verge of a major transformation to an entirely unprecedented and radically novel level and type of awareness, which research after research indicates is—to use common terms—systemic, unified, holistic, integral, inclusive, embracing, interwoven, interconnected. Let us be sure that not just our sciences but our humanities and spiritualities are part of that radical transformation. And thus let us take the very best of our paths of the Great Liberation into the modern and postmodern world, thereby preparing them for the leap into this new transformation as well. Buddhism would then be prepared to even more often offer humanity what it has always excelled at offering. And that is? When Fa-chang was dying, a squirrel screeched out on the temple roof. "It's just this," he said, "and nothing more."

# SELECTED BOOKS BY KEN WILBER

*Boomeritis: A Novel That Will Set You Free*
The story of a grad student's journey to self-discovery, combining brilliant scholarship with wicked parody. The novel targets one of the most stubborn obstacles to realizing the Integral vision: a disease of pluralism plus narcissism that Wilber calls "boomeritis" because it seems to plague the Baby Boomer generation most of all.

*A Brief History of Everything, 20th Anniversary Edition*
Join Ken Wilber on a breathtaking tour of time and the Kosmos—from the Big Bang right up to the eve of the twenty-first century. This accessible summary of Wilber's ideas has been expanding minds now for two decades, providing a kind of unified field theory of the universe and, along the way, treating a host of related issues from gender roles to multiculturalism, environmentalism, the meaning of the Internet, and more. This special anniversary edition contains, as an afterword, a conversation between the author and award-winning filmmaker Lana Wachowski (*Cloud Atlas*, the *Matrix* trilogy) in which we're offered an intimate glimpse into the evolution of Wilber's thinking and where he stands today.

*Grace and Grit: Spirituality and Healing in the Life and Death of Treya Killam Wilber*
The moving story of Ken's marriage to Treya and the five-year journey that took them through her illness, treatment, and eventual

death from breast cancer. Ken's wide-ranging commentary is combined with excerpts from Treya's personal journals.

*Integral Meditation: Mindfulness as a Way to Grow Up, Wake Up, and Show Up in Your Life*
Prepare to encounter your mind in a radically new way as Ken Wilber introduces Integral Mindfulness, a meditative approach based on Integral Theory and Practice. This leading-edge technique combines, for the first time in history, the ancient paths of meditation and mindfulness—or Waking Up—with modern research into psychological development and human evolution—Growing Up—resulting in a complete and powerfully effective method of personal transformation.

*Integral Spirituality: A Startling New Role for Religion in the Modern and Postmodern World*
A theory of spirituality that honors the truths of premodernity, modernity, and postmodernity—including the revolutions in science and culture—while incorporating the essential insights of the great religions.

*The Integral Vision: A Very Short Introduction to the Revolutionary Integral Approach to Life, God, the Universe, and Everything*
An accessible book for anyone who wants an easy introduction to Ken Wilber's thought and its practical applications, both personal and global. The key components of his Integral Approach—a tool for "making sense of everything"—are distilled here into a simple and elegant full-color presentation.

*The Religion of Tomorrow: A Vision for the Future of the Great Traditions—More Inclusive, More Comprehensive, More Complete*
A single purpose lies at the heart of all the great religious traditions: awakening to the astonishing reality of the true nature of ourselves and the universe. At the same time, through centuries of cultural accretion and focus on myth and ritual as ends in them-

selves, this core insight has become obscured. Here Ken Wilber provides a path for reenvisioning a religion of the future that acknowledges the evolution of humanity in every realm while remaining faithful to that original spiritual vision.

### Sex, Ecology, Spirituality: The Spirit of Evolution
The first volume of the Kosmos Trilogy and the book that introduced the 4-quadrant model. This tour de force of scholarship and vision traces the course of evolution from matter to life to mind (and possible higher levels), and describes the common patterns that evolution takes in all three domains. Wilber particularly focuses on how modernity and postmodernity relate to gender issues, psychotherapy, ecological concerns, and various liberation movements.

### A Theory of Everything: An Integral Vision for Business, Politics, Science, and Spirituality
A compact summary of the Integral Approach as a genuine "world philosophy," noteworthy because it includes many real-world applications in various fields. A popular choice for introductory reading, it is compact and succinct, with many hands-on examples.

### Trump and a Post-Truth World
The world is in turmoil. Democracies are reeling in the face of nihilism and narcissism. How, with so much antagonism, cynicism, and discord, can we mend the ruptures in our societies? In this provocative work, Wilber applies his Integral approach to explain how we arrived where we are and why there is cause for hope.

# INDEX